Flipping Houses With No Money Down: Three-Hour Crash Course

How to Flip Homes for Beginners, Attract Real Estate Investors, and Finance Projects Using Investment Capital

Edward Day

Table of Contents

Introduction

"Buying real estate is not only the best way, the quickest way, and the safest way, but the only way to become wealthy."
- Marshall Field

'Flipping' might sound like a trick that you could do on a trampoline as a kid, but it's arguably much more fun than that (and you're less likely to give your mother a heart attack while doing it). In the United States of America, the term 'flipping' is often used to refer to the buying and reselling of assets to make a profit. You can flip anything from retail products to cars, but the most profitable asset to flip by far is real estate. Flipping houses involves buying property, renovating or rehabbing it, and reselling it for a profit within a year of its initial purchase.

Flipping real estate might sound like a pipe dream to some, but the fact of the matter is that more than 200,000 residential properties are flipped by average Americans every single year. What's stopping you from joining them?

Not only are hundreds of thousands of Americans flipping homes every single year, but they're also making a lot of money doing it. ATTOM Data Solutions, one of the USA's leading property data and statistics companies, estimates that your average flipper makes about $65,000 per transaction (or a profit of 40% of the amount that they initially invested in the property). Jason Kidd says that aspiring house flippers need to flip at least two to seven houses per year if they want to make flipping property their full-time job (don't worry, I'm about to teach you how).

Many people make a living off of flipping houses, but some make millions, like Sidney Torres, Lin He, Jennifer Beadles, Frank Cava, and Armando Montelongo.

Sidney Torres is a real estate investor (and the host of the property-centric television series 'The Deed') who has made millions flipping houses. He was only earning about $40,000 per year when he first got interested in real estate, and soon had his heart set firmly on a property in New Orleans. The only problem was that the property's price tag was $40,000. Torres pleaded with his grandmother, who had always acted as a mentor to him, to lend him the capital that he required to make the purchase, but she had some requirements of her own.

She asked Torres to essentially submit a business plan, including time frames and financial analysis, before she would even consider discussing lending him that amount of money. Fortunately, she was impressed with his submissions and decided to help him. By the end of its renovation, Torres's first-ever investment property was worth more than $60,000 more than what he had originally paid for it, starting a landslide of real estate success. He currently has a net worth of about $300 million, proving once and for all that there's (a lot of) money to be made flipping houses.

Lin He bought a dilapidated mansion in Malibu for $985,000 three years ago and spent about 90 days renovating it and giving it a makeover. Just like Torres, he did a lot of work on the house himself, which helped him to keep his costs low. After three months of rehabilitation, he put the mansion back on the market for just under $2 million and managed to sell it for more than twice the price that he originally paid for it.

He says that even when taking into consideration the vast amount of work that he needed to have done on the house (which naturally came at a cost), he still managed to make a clean profit of nearly half a million dollars from the deal. He proves that you don't need to flip 20 houses every year to make a substantial profit if you're willing to hedge a bet on some more expensive properties.

Jennifer Beadles was a 21-year-old bookkeeper when she purchased her first home. She describes it as having needed quite a lot of work and rehabilitation, but because banks were offering zero-down loans, she decided to take the plunge anyway. It was this purchase that she says sparked her love for and interest in real estate and real estate development. Her newly-discovered passion drove her to apply for a vacancy as a financial administrator at a local building company. She got the job and immediately set out to learn everything that she possibly could about construction to improve her skills as a house flipper. Once she learned all that she believed that she could, she got her real estate license and committed herself fully to buying and selling property. Her net worth is currently over $1 million, and she enjoys the freedom that this wealth affords her to spend time with her husband and young daughter.

Frank Cava accepted a job as a construction manager in Florida straight out of university. One of the biggest drawing points to this position was the fact that the company offered its employees about $3,000 in financial relief if they chose to build a house using the company's services. Cava decided to do just that and built a sprawling suburban home of more than 2,500 square feet. The problem was that Cava was only earning a little bit more than $4,000 a month at a time, this isn't a problem in and of itself, but the mortgage on Cava's newly built home was $5,000, which presented a bit of a challenge.

He decided to circumvent this problem entirely by renting out every single room in his newly built mansion to friends and college students, even going as far as renting out his basement as a living space. While it might sound like a crazy idea, it ultimately paid off because it allowed Cava to keep his supersized starter home. Not only did he manage to keep it, but he also managed to refinance it to purchase his first investment property and then sold both to buy his first landmark property for $850,000 (an investment that he ultimately made nearly $600,000 on). He currently has a net worth of more than $10 million (although the exact figure is unknown) and runs his own very successful property development venture.

Armando Montelongo, a real estate guru and the host of a television series called 'Flip This House,' spent most of his early adulthood surviving off of food stamps, living in a garage, and struggling to make ends meet. He was stuck in the cycle of poverty, and he knew it—but he also knew that he wanted to escape it. Out of desperation, Montelongo approached four multi-millionaire investors and begged them to mentor him to help him escape his current financial position. All four agreed and within a couple of months, with their guidance, Montelongo purchased and moved into his very first 3,500 square foot house. Once Montelongo tasted success, he didn't back off. He kept executing bigger and bigger purchases and sales and continues to do so to this day. His net worth is currently more than $50 million, consequently his financial woes are a thing of the past.

If these five average-Joes-turned-millionaires can do it, so can you (even if, like Montelongo, you're currently living off of welfare). Financial freedom is achievable for everyone, you simply need to be determined to learn and determined to succeed. Nobody should have to live paycheck to paycheck, nobody should have to worry about providing for their children, nobody should have to count their cents to spoil their spouse, and nobody should have to lie awake at night worrying about cash. I don't want that for you, and I'm sure that you don't want it for yourself either. If you stick with this book to its end, I'm going to teach you how to make millions, I'll show you how you too can be free.

It's not just those who are hoping to make millions that get involved in flipping houses, those that already have millions like to make even more by doing it too. Adam Levine, the lead singer of Maroon 5 and previously a judge on the television series called 'The Voice,' is known to purchase million-dollar houses, renovate them, and to resell them for a profit of millions. He sold $35 million worth in real estate in 2017 and has since reinvested in several different properties.

Vanilla Ice, the guy who rapped that super catchy song, 'Ice Ice Baby' in 1989, famously has a passion for flipping houses and has since been offered his own television series ('The Vanilla Ice Project') that centers around the art (and science) of flipping houses. He has been doing it for about 15 years now, and these days the profits generated by it are his main source of income (and he doesn't seem to be living too uncomfortably).

Jeremy Renner, who plays Hawkeye in The Avengers, is quite a prominent house flipper. He proved his worth as a real estate mogul in 2013 when he reported having earned more than $17 million over a three-year period from flipping alone. The house flipping bug has even bitten Ellen DeGeneres, and it's reported that she has spent nearly $150 million on property over the course of her career. If flipping houses is good enough for Ellen DeGeneres and Hawkeye, it's certainly good enough for you. Joining their ranks could see you joining them in the millionaire club too, and who doesn't want that? If you follow my advice, you could be sipping cocktails with Vanilla Ice at property viewings in no time.

It's no surprise that house flipping is such a popular stream of income. It offers investors the chance to make millions, without requiring them to understand any fancy financial figures that other forms of investing, like stock trading, does. You also don't need to commit all of your time to it, you can hold down a full-time job while also benefiting from the side income offered by it. Renovating a broken-down home from years gone by, can also give you an exceptional sense of fulfillment and accomplishment, which is something a lot of us don't get from our nine-to-five jobs.

You would have to be crazier than a rabid circus clown to not want to get involved in the real estate market by flipping houses when it has proven itself to be such an effective way to generate cash. I mean, who doesn't want to be a millionaire? Especially when it's so easy.

Who I Am

I bet you're sitting there wondering, *'Who is this guy who says that he's going to change my life and make me a millionaire? I don't even know him!'* Well, allow me to introduce myself, I'm Edward Day and I know a thing or two about making money. Sure, I have university degrees and a sizable bank account to back up that statement, but they're not what I'm talking about. You see, I used to be just like you, I know what you're going through—but I also know how to help you through it.

I went off and worked as an accountant straight out of university. I had a bachelor's degree in accounting behind my name, the world was my oyster, and I believed that I was exactly where I needed to be. Unfortunately, it got old really quickly and I soon began to feel like I had to be destined for more. I mean, surely living isn't just about living paycheck-to-paycheck while working nine-to-five, Monday through Friday. Surely it was about traveling, spending time with my family, and making memories (all things that I was struggling to find time for).

It was around this time that I met one of my first mentors (now a close friend), a Forex trader who paid me for my services as an accountant. Our professional relationship was still in its infancy when he invited me along to a Forex seminar with him. I went, and it changed my life. It made me realize that there were more ways to make money than sitting behind a desk for eight or nine hours every day. I suddenly had this epiphany that I could make my money work for me instead of spending all of my time working for it. From there on out, I got involved in Forex trading, completed an additional bachelor's degree in economics, and made a decent sum. But I knew I could make even more—which is when I started investing in real estate.

I haven't had a nine-to-five office gig for more than twelve years, and I've successfully been making a consistent return of 12%, per annum, on all of my property investments, which has really helped me to get ahead. By the end of this book, I will teach you all of the secrets I've learned over the years, and you'll be well on your way to becoming a millionaire too.

Who You Are

If you've picked up this book, you're likely an ambitious individual who wants more from life. You're clearly determined too, if you're willing to dedicate your time to learning a new skill to improve your lifestyle. I like ambitious, determined individuals because they're the kind of people who get things done, and who manage to affect real-life changes in their lives for their own betterment. Both of these qualities will help you to manifest your dreams and will guide you on your journey to success. If you're both brave and determined, you're also likely to be brave and courageous. You certainly need to be brave to step away from everything that you know to chase a new dream, which is exactly what you're doing right now.

You're likely someone that has (or has had) an unfulfilling, nine-to-five job that made you realize that you'd prefer to own your own time and to work for yourself. Who needs a boss anyway? It's just that you might not know where to start in order to achieve the kind of financial freedom that you need to bid your role as an employee farewell. You're also probably a bit smarter than the average person, and you've realized that there has to be a way to break free from 'the system.'

While ambition, determination, bravery, courage and intelligence are all a solid part of the recipe for a successful house flipper, you'll need a little bit more than that to make millions. Experts have narrowed down the list of personality traits that you need to be successful at flipping houses by studying those who have already made millions from doing it. Some of the traits and characteristics include; being disciplined, having organizational skills, being financially frugal, being practical, being open to advice, receiving feedback gracefully, remaining humble, being realistic, being business-oriented, persistence, and being willing to take risks.

You need to be disciplined because flipping houses takes a lot of hard work. If you're going to be doing it on a budget, you might even need to do a lot of the physical renovations and improvements to the property yourself, consequently you need to be willing to go to a property, every day, and to spend a couple of hours essentially doing what a physical laborer would do (for example, painting, woodwork, tiling, carpeting, or gardening). Being willing to consistently and regularly put some (literal) blood, sweat, and tears into your investment property takes a lot of discipline, but luckily I know that you're up for it.

Additionally, you need to be organized and willing to become even more so. Flipping houses means dealing with a lot of time pressure, handling ten thousand different quotes from numerous contractors, ordering supplies and building materials (in their correct quantities and at the best price possible), hiring and managing laborers, and handling any rates and taxes that may be applicable to your investment properties. That's a lot of administrative work. If you don't have a filing cabinet yet, I suggest that you get one.

You need to be financially frugal to keep your costs low. The purpose of house flipping is entirely nullified if you buy a house for $200,000, spend $100,000 revamping it, and then sell it again for $300,000—because then your profit margin would be absolutely zero. The goal is to buy a house for $200,000, to spend $50,000 renovating it, and to sell it for $300,000. But to do this you need to spend as little money as possible. This is generally achievable, by doing some of the physical labor yourself, buying discounted building materials, and buying in bulk.

You also need to be practical and realistic, or you will be perpetually disappointed. Being impatient with yourself in the beginning stages of your journey to financial freedom, because you've set impossible goals, is setting yourself up for failure. Giving yourself leeway to learn and to make mistakes is absolutely essential if you intend on flipping houses with your mental health still intact.

It is also absolutely essential that you learn how to take feedback (even negative feedback) and build on it. Your mentors and potential buyers will all have opinions on your progress and efficiency as a house flipper, and you better bet that they'll probably give them to you every chance that they get. It's important that you learn from these comments instead of taking offense to them, a skill that can take some time to hone. However, if you don't learn to do it, you'll find yourself becoming disheartened in no time when there's really no reason to be. Growing a thicker skin will be a crucial part of your journey.

The downfall of many investors (in both real estate and in the stock market) is vanity. They get a taste of success, which goes to their head, and then they start making silly investment decisions and chasing that high. The ability to remain humble is crucial to any house flipper because you will undoubtedly be successful, which means that you will definitely be tempted to go all-in or to make impractical investments.

Another important characteristic that all great house flippers share, is a business-oriented mind. You can't go into this thinking that you'll do it as a hobby, because that is setting yourself up for failure. You need to view flipping houses as your business and your full-time occupation. Of course, this also means that you need to manage your finances like you would those of a business and that you need to set goals for yourself like you would for a growing business.

If you want to be a successful house flipper, you need to be willing to take risks. Every investment that you make is essentially a risk, the goal is to take calculated risks. Of course, taking calculated risks still means taking risks. Not everybody has the grit to live with the uncertainty that comes with flipping houses for a living, however, I'm certain that you're the kind of person who will be able to dive into this headfirst, without becoming overwhelmed. You've already proven yourself to be a bit of a gambler by even considering taking up house flipping, this means that you're exactly the kind of person who is likely to become wealthy from doing it (or so the experts say, anyway).

The final trait that all successful house flippers share is persistence. If you want to make millions, you need persistence to the power of one million. Sometimes the going gets tough when you're the only one responsible for your income, and it isn't all coming in the form of a reliable paycheck. Not only can getting started be financially frustrating, but you're likely to suffer a loss or two (or three) in the beginning too. It can be emotionally frustrating. You need a good dose of persistence if you're going to see your dream of flipping houses through, even when it's not going exactly like you hoped it would.

If you feel that you embody a few of these traits (shared by hundreds of real estate millionaires), then you're in the right place, and I can definitely help you to widen the girth of your bank account. If you feel that you might be lacking a couple of these traits, that's okay too—we'll work on garnering them, together.

How This Book is About to Change Your Life (and Make You Millions)

I'm sure that people have made a lot of promises to you over the course of your life, and I bet many of those have not been kept, as you might have hoped. Most promises aren't worth the paper they're written on (or the breath that was spent uttering them), but this one is different—I promise that if you stick with this book until its end, you'll have the opportunity to live the kind of life that you only thought was possible in your fantasies. That's a promise that you can rely on and trust, because thousands of people have made millions by using the kind of information and techniques discussed in this book.

Many people feel that earning millions is just a pipe dream, but there's absolutely no truth to this. There are nearly 47 million millionaires in the world right now. This means that there are ten million more millionaires alive right now than there are people living in Canada. In fact, the United States of America has more than 18 million millionaires living in it at this very moment. That means that five out of every 100,000 American citizens are millionaires. There's absolutely nothing stopping you from being one of those people. If being a millionaire was impossible, nobody would be able to achieve it.

Over the course of the next six chapters, I'm going to discuss the basics of house flipping, real estate jargon, and the different kinds of house flipping methodologies; and I'm going to teach you how to spot undervalued properties, how to keep your costs low, how to budget for your new venture, how to avoid common pitfalls, how to garner some of the traits commonly associated with successful house flippers, how to market your first investment, and how to acquire financial assistance.

In essence, I'm going to be providing you with a step-by-step guide to house flipping that will guide you from this point onwards up until the point that you resell your first investment property. You don't need to go through any of this feeling lost or alone because I will be there with you all of the way.

Chapter 1:

Understanding What 'Flipping Houses' Actually Means

As I said in the introduction, flipping houses is essentially the practice of buying investment properties, fixing them up, and reselling them for a profit - all within a twelve-month period. I wish it was as simple as it sounds, but unfortunately there's a little more to it than just that. You'll need to learn how to spot houses that are selling for less than they're worth, learn what kind of repairs and rehabilitation needs to be done on them (and how to manage the costs while doing so), and figure out how to get the most out of reselling them. Luckily, I'm about to teach all of that to you. Unfortunately, I need to teach you the basics before we can get to that.

House flipping has been around for as long as homeownership has, although it experienced a massive surge in popularity during the 1980s. The United States of America (along with most of the rest of the world) experienced a terrible financial recession in 1981 and 1982 which saw the closure of many businesses, which in turn led to unprecedented levels of unemployment. The sheer number of people who lost their jobs during this period consequently led to an increase in home foreclosures that caused house prices to plummet across the board.

While most Americans despaired, some savvy investors saw an opportunity to make millions and started buying up some of these incredibly discounted properties. Of course, the economy soon started recovering, which meant that those who had been clever enough to scoop up property during the recession were left smiling all the way to the bank, as they were able to resell their investments for hefty profits. This phenomenon essentially birthed the modern popularity of house flipping and in turn, spawned a whole host of television series centered around it like Masters of Flip, Flipping Vegas, Flip Men, Flip This House, The Adam Carolla Project, and Flipping Out.

Today, the practice of flipping houses makes up 10% of all of the real estate transactions performed in the United States of America, with approximately 150,000 properties being flipped every year. Luckily, this means that you're about to enter a well-established community of real estate investors where you'll find a wealth of communal help, guidance, and information at your disposal.

Getting to Know the Lingo

House flippers have a language of their own. Your ability to network with other real estate investors and moguls heavily depends on whether you're capable of speaking this language. Luckily it's much, much easier than learning a conventional additional language like German or French, but that doesn't mean that you should neglect your study of it. This little dictionary of house flipping terms will have you well on your way to being fluent in real estate lingo, but you should still invest some time in reading other books and articles on the subject to get a feeling for how these terms are used in practice.

30-, 60-, and 90-Pre-nod list: These are lists compiled by research and data companies that contain the details of homeowners who have missed one, two, or three consecutive mortgage payments, but who have not yet been foreclosed on. You might be wondering, *'Well, why would I need that kind of information?'*, but the answer is really simple. Homeowners who have missed a couple of payments are likely to be in some kind of financial trouble, consequently they might be looking to sell their property at a discounted price to avoid racking up even more debt. You could use a 30-, 60-, and 90-pre-nod list to contact these homeowners and find out whether they'd be willing to sell their property to you.

The biggest benefit of these lists is that they reveal the details of homeowners who are about to be foreclosed on, and not those of homeowners who have already been foreclosed on. Once a homeowner is foreclosed on, that foreclosure becomes public knowledge, so every Tom, Dick, and Harry will be in contact with them, making offers that you might not be able to match. The general public doesn't know the details of homeowners who are about to be foreclosed on, this means that contacting them at this point gives you a bit of a head start. Unfortunately, these kinds of lists aren't free (if they were, everybody would use them) and need to be purchased from vendors like My Lead Dog, Citracado, or Data List Leader.

After-repair value (ARV): This term means exactly what it says on the label. It is the value of an investment property after you've bought it, rehabilitated it, and fixed it up. It's important to try to work out what a property's ARV will be before purchasing it, to make sure that your profit margin (the difference between the price you're paying for it and the price you'll be selling it for) is large enough to warrant all of the time and effort that you will have to put in.

Appraisal: This term refers to an estimation of an investment property's value that is made by a qualified real estate guru, who is entirely independent (and thus has no relationship with the owner or the possible buyer of the property). Appraisers work out the value of an investment property by considering its size, location, curb appeal, the prices of other comparable properties, and the strength of the housing market. You won't be able to get a mortgage on a potential property if it hasn't been appraised by a qualified appraiser. In the USA, appraisers need to meet several requirements and pass a board exam to be registered with The Appraisal Foundation. This allows them to offer their services professionally.

Assignment: This one is a little complicated, but bear with me. An assignment is when you sign a contract of sale to purchase an investment property, only to sell the buying rights of the property to a different house flipper. This is done before the sale officially goes through putting the property in your name. It might sound a little convoluted, but it is actually a fantastic way to make a series of small profits (and one that is often utilized by wholesalers, who I'll describe a little later on). An example of assignment would be if you purchased a run-down property for $150,000, only to reassign its buying rights to a different house flipper for $160,000. This transaction would place you at the receiving end of $10,000, even though the price that the sellers originally wanted for the place was only

$150,000. It boils down to getting to promising properties before anyone else does, even if you do not intend to renovate them and do a full flip with them yourself.

Back-up status: Sometimes an investment property will remain on the market even if a contract of sale has been signed pertaining to its sale. This is normally done when the seller or real estate agent believes that the sale might fall through, this belief could be based on a number of factors, but is usually founded on the idea that a potential buyer might struggle to get a mortgage or loan. By keeping the property on the market, other potential buyers can continue to view it and make offers on it (forming a queue behind the signing buyer whose ability to acquire the property is being questioned). If the sale falls through as was feared, then another potential buyer can immediately step-in and restart the process.

Bene: This term stems from the word 'beneficiary.' You'll probably hear it used at a foreclosure auction if the property in question doesn't sell during the auction, because at that point, it will go to the 'bene' (the beneficiary who put the foreclosure auction into motion, usually the company that issued the mortgage on the property). The bene can then decide what to do with the property, some may choose to keep it, but it's more likely that they'll put it up for sale at an even lower price than the minimum bid that was required at auction.

Bird dog (also known as a 'real estate jobber' or as a 'deal scout'): Remember what I said about 30-, 60-, and 90-pre-nod lists? Well, 'bird dog' is the term that is used to refer to the people or companies who, for a fee, draw up these lists or hunt down similar kinds of leads for house flippers. This term refers to companies like My Lead Dog, Citracado, or Data List Leader, for example.

Buying costs: These are costs that are associated with buying a property that are charged over and above its actual purchase price. Some of these fees and charges include inspection costs, brokerage fees, lending fees, and title work. You should consider a property's buying costs to make sure that it still fits into your budget, even when they're included before you make an offer to purchase.

Closing: The 'closing' (or end) of a property transaction, takes place when its title deed and ownership is transferred from the seller or mortgage holder to the new buyer. You can only offer the property up for sale again once the transaction has been closed, and you may need to hold back on any renovations and repairs until such time.

Construction contingency: This is a term that is used to refer to a sum of money (normally expressed as a percentage of the overall cost of construction) that a construction company might ask you to reserve in case they end up going over their initial quote to finish the job satisfactorily. It is usually used to cover any unexpected costs or complications that may occur above and beyond the quoted construction. You might want to consider putting away a bit of money for construction contingency, even if you're not making use of a construction company, just in case you yourself end up running into costs that you didn't anticipate running into.

Counteroffer: You make a seller an 'offer' when you ask to buy their property for a certain sum. Normally, you'd make an offer that is below the price that the seller is asking to try to get a discount on their asking price. A seller might accept this offer, they might reject it entirely, or they might make a counteroffer that is more than what you offered, but that is still less than their original asking price. An example of a counteroffer would be if you offered to buy a house listed as $200,000 for $150,000, and the seller comes back to you and tells you that while they're unable to accept $150,000, they would be willing to take $180,000 for the property. You then have the choice to accept this counter offer, to reject it, or to make another counteroffer of your own. Following on the earlier example, you might counteroffer for a second time by offering the seller $170,000 instead of $180,000.

Covenants: This is a term that is used to refer to rules that are set by an area's Homeowners' Association that apply to all of the homes and homeowners that find themselves in that specific area. They often regulate the appearance of the houses falling under their jurisdiction by stating that they need to be painted a certain color or be built in a certain style. It is important to check whether any covenants apply to any properties that you're planning on flipping, because this might affect the kind of renovations that you'll be allowed to do.

Distressed property: This term is used to refer to properties that have been reclaimed by the company that issued their mortgages, or to properties that have been claimed by their owners' creditors (people who are owed money by their owners). Both of the aforementioned parties will probably want to offload the property as soon as possible to recover some of their money, you'll likely be able to pick up these properties for an absolute steal.

Dollhouse: This is a term used to refer to potential investment properties that only need some minor aesthetic repairs in order for you to be able to resell them for a profit. They're a good choice for someone who wants to flip a property as quickly as possible or who doesn't have a lot of money to spend on renovating the place.

Earnest Money Deposit: This is a sum of money (normally about $1,000) that some sellers offer buyers when they make them an offer to show them that they're serious about the transaction, and that they have the money on hand to cover the offered amount (although this isn't always necessarily true). You are not obligated to offer sellers an earnest money deposit although some house flippers believe that doing so will entice the buyer to accept your offer instead of rejecting it outright or making a counteroffer.

Escrow: When you buy a property and pay its asking price, that money gets put into 'escrow' and is kept there until the transaction is concluded, at which point it is paid out to the seller. It is held in escrow by an independent third company, like a law firm or the title company, so you don't have to be concerned about it being misappropriated. If the sale does not go through, for whatever reason, the funds held in escrow will be paid back to you again.

Haircut: This is a term used to refer to a potential investment property that only needs some gardening or landscaping work done before you'll be able to resell it for a profit. Increasing these properties' values is usually as easy as mowing the lawn, pulling out a couple of weeds, and trimming the hedges. Haircut properties amplify all of the benefits of dollhouse properties tenfold, offering their investors a way to make a quick buck without having to spend too much money to be able to do it.

Hard-money lenders: This is a term that is used to refer to individuals or companies that are willing to lend money to real estate investors to enable them to flip a property. These lenders generally pay out loans much faster (and with far fewer strings attached) than traditional mortgage facilitators, like banks do. While it's much easier to secure a loan from hard-money lenders, their interest rates tend to be substantially higher than those of traditional financial institutions. You should think long and hard before making use of a hard-money lender because their exorbitant interest rates can take quite a bite out of the profit of the sale of an investment property.

Homeowners' association dues: If the property that you've just purchased falls under the jurisdiction of a homeowners' association, then you might find yourself having to pay them a sum of money either monthly or annually in exchange for the services that they offer (like maintaining public pool facilities, communal areas, your garden, and the area's waste and garbage management system). If you're planning on flipping a house that falls in an area that is controlled by a homeowner's association, you should make sure that you calculate any homeowners' association dues that you might have to pay while you're renovating it into your overall costs.

HUD home: This term refers to a property that has been placed up for sale by the Department of Federal Housing and Urban Development (HUD) because its owner was foreclosed on because they failed to make their Federal Housing Association (FHA) loan payments in time. HUD homes are usually put on the market for well below their actual market value. They offer house flippers a stellar opportunity to increase their profit margins.

Multi-family property: This is a term used in property listings that refers to a property that has multiple living units (and that can consequently accommodate numerous families). Examples of multi-family properties are apartment buildings, homes with an apartment attached or with an additional apartment on the property, duplexes, and triplexes. You generally need to put a lot more work into multi-family properties in order to renovate them simply because there are more living units to renovate, but your possible profit margin on properties of this kind is also normally larger.

Pending status: A property transaction reaches the point known as 'pending status' when you make an offer on a property that gets accepted by the seller of the property, who then consequently, closes themselves off to any further offers from outside parties in final acceptance of yours. A transaction reaches pending status just before you're expected to deliver payment or loan guarantees.

Pre-qualification: Most lenders and financial institutions are willing to pre-qualify you for a loan of up to a certain amount in writing if you're willing to submit some documents pertaining to your assets, income, and liabilities to them in order for them to work out your financial status. Sellers are normally more willing to accept offers that have been made by buyers who can either pay in cash or who have pre-qualified for a loan because they know that the transaction is likely to proceed quickly from that point onward (instead of being delayed by the financial problems of buyers who might not be able to secure funding after making an offer).

Recording fees: This term refers to a sum of money that you have to pay your local county in order for them to register you as the new owner of a property that you have just purchased. You should definitely take recording fees into account when you're considering the overall cost of flipping a property although they shouldn't be a deciding factor because they normally don't exceed about $100.

Selling costs: This is a term that is used to refer to the costs that you might incur as a seller once you put your investment home on the market. It includes things like seller assisted closing costs, commission fees that are owed to real estate agents, and warranties. You should try to keep your selling costs as low as possible to ensure that your profit margins remain reasonable in size.

Single family residence: This is a term that is normally used in property listings that refers to a property that only contains a single living unit. As a house flipper, you'll mostly be dealing with these kinds of properties because single residential homes are a house flipper's bread and butter.

Staging: You 'stage' a property when you decorate and fill it with furnishings just before offering it for viewing to the general public. The purpose of staging a property is to make it look more appealing to potential buyers. Fashionable furniture that is strategically placed makes a much better impression than an empty house does because it allows your buyers to picture themselves living there.

Sweat equity: This is a term that is used to refer to the work that a house flipper puts into a property before reselling it and stems from the common quip, 'blood, sweat, and tears.' Some properties, like those that are very dilapidated, will require more sweat equity than others before they're resellable.

Under contract: A property is said to be 'under contract' once you've made an offer on it that has been accepted in writing by the seller. It is called thus because once a seller accepts an offer, they are contractually obligated to continue with the transaction. You can be pretty sure that your purchase of a property will go through once you reach this point (as long as you have the funding needed to back up your offer).

Weekend warrior: This is a term that is used to refer to house flippers who do not make flipping houses their full-time occupation. Instead, these individuals tend to approach flipping houses as a casual hobby that they take part in alongside their actual job. Your chances of being successful as a house flipper are greatly decreased if you approach house flipping in this way, this is because flipping houses requires all of your time and your full attention if you want to be able to maximize your profits.

Wholesaler: This term is used to refer to house flippers who buy and sell an incredibly large number of properties when compared to your average house flipper. They're capable of increasing their sales volume because they generally do not do any repairs to the properties that they purchase. They simply acquire them for a bargain price and then resell them for a couple of grand more to a house flipper, who is willing to put in all of the work that they're not in order to resell it for its full potential price. In essence, wholesalers are house flippers who sell houses to other house flippers.

Important House Flipping Formulas

Luckily for most, house flipping doesn't require a physicists' level of understanding of mathematics in order for you to be successful in it, but that doesn't mean that there aren't any numbers involved in flipping houses at all. In fact, there are only two formulas that you really need to commit to memory, and they're fortunately relatively straight forward. These two formulas belong to the '70% rule' and the 'maximum price rule.'

The 70% rule is an unwritten rule that all successful house flippers follow. It states that you should absolutely never pay more for a property than 70% of its after repair value, with all of your repair and renovation costs already subtracted from it. This rule helps house flippers to keep their profit margins large enough in size for flipping to remain a profitable exercise.

It is expressed as:

(After repair value × 0.7) - repair costs = maximum purchase price

An example of the 70% rule in action would be if you purchased an investment property for $200,000 and spent $50,000 on its repairs. Then you would need to sell it for at least $357,142.86 in order to make a profit that aligns itself with the 70% rule. You can reach this conclusion by slightly tweaking the equation above in the following way:

(After repair value×0.7) - $50,000 = $200,000

After repair value×0.7= $200,000 + $50,000

After repair value = $250,000 ÷0.7

After repair value = $357,142.86

The maximum purchase price formula can also be used to help you to deduce how much money you should spend on an investment property's purchase price. It is calculated by taking the property's after repair value and subtracting any costs (like buying costs, the profit that you want to make off of the sale, financing costs, selling costs, holding costs, and repair costs) from it.

An example of this would be if you were trying to work out the maximum purchase price of a property that's after repair value is about $300,000, and you'd like to make about $50,000 when reselling it, and that's buying costs, repair costs, selling costs, holding costs, and financing costs equal about $40,000. The maximum price that you should pay for such a property is about $210,000. This can also be expressed as a formula as:

After repair value - the profit you'd like to make off of the sale - costs = maximum purchase price

Using these two formulas will help you to determine how much you need to sell for in order to remain profitable, and how much you can afford to buy for while still keeping your profit margin a reasonable size.

Your Legal Obligations as a House Flipper

Nobody likes reading the disclaimer (I mean, we all just click 'accept,' don't we?), but when it's your money on the line, it's important that you familiarize yourself with state and federal laws pertaining to house flipping.

First, one of the requirements of Federal Housing Administration (FHA) loans is that property that is

purchased may not be sold within three months of its date of purchase. Many house flippers are blissfully unaware of this clause because they're blinded by the FHA's dazzlingly low-interest rates and down payments, but it's definitely something to be mindful of if you're hoping to flip a property in less time. Despite this definite downside, FHA loans remain popular because they're so easily accessible and affordable.

If you have a credit score of more than 580, you qualify for an FHA loan of up to 96.5%. If you fall into this credit bracket, you could get a loan of up to $193,000 on a home that's worth $200,000, which means that you'll only need a deposit of $7,000. Luckily, FHA loans aren't only for those with stellar credit scores. If your credit score is 579 or lower (but not lower than 510), then you could still qualify for an FHA loan of up to 90%. If you were to take on one of these loans, you would be able to get a loan of up to $180,000 on a property that is worth $200,000, consequently you'd only need to make an initial payment of $20,000.

There are undoubtedly several benefits to taking out an FHA loan, but other than the 90 days in which you won't be allowed to sell the property, you'll also be required to submit supporting documentation to the FHA if you manage to sell your investment property for twice of its original purchase price (or more) within five months of its acquisition. These regulations were put in place in an attempt to crack down on money laundering, and are in no way intended to discourage the practice of house flipping, so although you'll have to abide by them if you take out an FHA loan, you don't have to feel like a bandit if you do legitimately manage to flip a property for 100% profit with five months (you just need to be able to prove that it was truly improved while you owned it, increasing its value, and that the buyer who purchased it is a legitimate buyer). If you made use of a different loan or your own capital to purchase property, then these time frames and regulations do not apply to you.

It's also important to be mindful of the fact that you could be held financially liable for any material defects to a property that you flipped if you were aware of the defect or tried to conceal it from potential buyers (in fact, you'll be punished far more severely in most states if you malevolently tried to hide a defect). Buyers won't be able to sue you if this defect hasn't caused them significant financial damage or if they should have been able to spot it from their own inspection of the property. On the other hand, if you buy an investment property with the hope of flipping it, but a week or two down the line you notice that it has a serious material defect, then you can sue whoever sold the property to you (along with potentially being able to hold the estate agent and home inspector liable too). Examples of material defects are serious water leaks in roofs, structural problems with the foundation, and improper wiring or plumbing. Considering all of the aforementioned, it's important to declare any defects that affect your investment property to potential buyers (even if you don't necessarily consider them to be particularly serious) to avoid being held liable later. You should also have any property that you're considering investing in inspected by a qualified, recognized home inspector to ensure that you don't end up buying any duds that'll cost you more money than they're worth in the long run.

Another potential problem that can arise is losses incurred because of lawsuits affecting the house that the previous owner is involved in (for example, they may have filed for bankruptcy and may have creditors who are looking to take ownership of the house because of debt incurred). A lawsuit of this nature can halt a property transaction in its tracks, and even reverse it, even after money has exchanged hands. Although this doesn't technically represent a legal obligation imposed on you, you should consider it a necessity to guard against any possible losses that may be suffered in this way. Fortunately, it's relatively easy to avoid falling into this trap because all you need to do to dodge it entirely, is to take out title insurance.

Taking out title insurance as the new potential owner of the property indemnifies you from a number of possible liabilities; it insures that the person selling the property to you really is its rightful owner (and thus has the right to sell it), and it guarantees you a payout should a major undisclosed defect be found affecting the property after the sale has been concluded. The four most popular title insurance issuing companies in the United States of America are the Stewart Information Services Corporation, Fidelity National Financial, the Old Republic International Corporation, and the First American Financial Corporation.

House flipping isn't highly regulated so, as long as you don't purposefully mislead potential buyers, it's unlikely that you'll get into any trouble with the law while doing it. It's infinitely more important to ensure that you're not the one being purposefully misled by sellers in order to avoid suffering any unnecessary financial losses.

Chapter 2:

Becoming Knowledgeable

While it's definitely important to commit some important house flipping terms to memory, and while it'll definitely help you to make more money if you're able to make sense of some of the most commonly used house flipping formulas, all of that means nothing if you don't know how to get the ball rolling. A lot of similar books gloss over the process involved in an actual flip, depriving readers of the opportunity to learn how to complete a trade from step one, but for the sake of learning, I'm going to teach you everything from how to pick your first investment property to how to sell it. By the end of this chapter, you should feel prepared to renovate your first flip property.

Of course, education is a never-ending journey. Some of you will undoubtedly be content with the information covered in this book, but for those of you who would like to learn more about the art of house flipping, there are five books that have been revered as scripture to house flippers that I can highly recommend. They are *Fix and Flip Your Way to Financial Freedom* by Mark Ferguson, *The Real Estate Rehab Investing Bible* by Paul Esajian, *50 Real Estate Investing Calculations* by Michael Lantrip, *The Business of Flipping*

Homes by William Bronchick, and *FLIP* by Clay Davis and Rick Villani.

Fix and Flip Your Way to Financial Freedom by Mark Ferguson, is just the book for you if you're interested in learning how to pull off multiple flips at once. Ferguson explains how to juggle up to 10 investment properties at once and how to maximize your profits by upping your negotiation game. This book is all about teaching you how to run your house flipping operation like a business, all whilst teaching you the gift of the gab (a skill that definitely comes in handy when you make a living off the real estate market).

The Real Estate Rehab Investing Bible by Paul Esajian, contains Esajian's highly coveted seven-step house flipping program. His followers swear that following it pretty much guarantees you success, even if you are a complete beginner. The only downside to this book is the fact that Esajian is all about flipping houses without lifting a finger, which means that a large part of it is dedicated to the topic of how to best utilize and negotiate with contractors. Unfortunately, this means that it's not necessarily the perfect guide for someone who is looking to do a lot of the renovating and rehabilitation themselves.

If some of the formulas mentioned in Chapter One made your head spin, but you'd still like to master them (or at the very least fully understand them), then you should consider reading *50 Real Estate Investing Calculations* by Michael Lantrip. A lot of us developed a deep-seated hatred for mathematics in high school, so it's entirely possible that you recoil at the mere thought of having to do a calculation, but there's really no reason to avoid the financial mathematics that is involved in house flipping. They're incredibly easy and straightforward, and you should be able to fully grasp them all with just a few minutes of study every day. Being literate in financial mathematics can set you apart from your fellow house flippers, and learning to apply it could see you joining the ranks of some of the world's most successful real estate investors. Additionally, the digital version of this book offers readers two dozen different pre-programmed calculators to work out applicable financial values quickly and easily.

The Business of Flipping Homes by William Bronchick is for your more seasoned house flippers. It doesn't cover the basics as well as the aforementioned books because it assumes a relative amount of knowledge on the part of its readers, but that doesn't mean that you shouldn't read it. In fact, Bronchick's book is a fantastic option once you feel that you fully understand the main principles behind house flipping. Bronchick covers the usual topics, like which kinds of homes and suburbs he believes to be most profitable, but then moves on to discuss some of the most common mistakes that house flippers make that can potentially rob them of thousands (if not hundreds of thousands) of dollars. It's this discussion on possible pitfalls that is the most valuable to real estate investors who are still learning the ropes.

FLIP, by Clay Davis and Rick Villani of HomeFixers, was a New York Times bestseller in 2008, its year of publication. It's the best possible guidebook (other than this one, of course) for aspiring house flippers and real estate investors. It covers all of the basics, but is probably most revered for its discussions on renovation and rehabilitation that are incredibly thorough but easy to digest. If you're looking to learn a bit more about how to get hands on with fixing up your investment property, then *FLIP* is more than likely just the book you need.

If you're more of an audio-visual learner, you might prefer to improve your knowledge of house flipping by subscribing to a couple of YouTube channels that post content specifically relating to real estate investments and the art of the flip. The two YouTube channels that I most highly recommend are, No Nonsense Chris and Extreme House Flipping.

No Nonsense Chris has been posting tips and tricks videos relating to house flipping for nearly a decade.

This channel is run by Christopher Cioffi of No Nonsense Real Estate who tactfully covers every and any topic that you can imagine, from how shower head height affects your chances of making a sale, to tips on how to get the best possible appraisal for your investment property (consequently increasing your profit margins). Many viewers enjoy Cioffi's straightforward approach to house flipping, and he makes sure to explain all of his topics in a way that is easily digestible for your average Joe. If you want to get straight down into the nitty-gritty instead of wasting time on formalities, then No Nonsense Chris is probably the perfect YouTube channel for you.

Extreme House Flipping is a YouTube channel run by HouseBarons, two brothers who make a living off of flipping houses with nearly zero outside help from hired workers and contractors. They've made use of this hands-on approach to make a myriad of do-it-yourself videos on how to do repairs and make improvements to your new investment property. They've been publishing videos for nearly eight years, some of their most popular ones are "Home Painting Tips to Make Painting Quicker and Easier," "How to Repair a Garden Hose," "Foundation Repair: How to Fix Foundation Cracks," and "How To Set A Fence Post in Concrete." If you're looking to keep your costs low by doing most of the work yourself, you should definitely head over to Extreme House Flipping to catch a few tips.

In the end, how knowledgeable you'll become on the topic of repairs, renovation, and house flipping in general, depends entirely upon how much work you're willing to put in. If you're willing to make studying the art of the flip your life's work, you'll be an absolute guru in no time.

How to Read a Property Listing

A property listing is how sellers advertise the properties that they're selling. They are often placed online, in magazines, in newspapers, and are sent to the Multiple Listing Service (which is a database of homes and properties for sale all around the world). Getting to know house flipping lingo might not be enough to teach you how to read a property listing because real estate agents have a lingo all their own too. Luckily you don't need to learn to speak it fluently, you only need to learn a few key phrases that are likely to appear on listings. Some of these phrases and abbreviations are:

DOM: This is an abbreviation of the term 'days on market.' Days on market refers to how many days have passed since the first day that the property was advertised for sale. This value is incredibly useful to house flippers because it's a good measuring staff for how desperate the owner will be to sell the property. On average, most American homes spend between 60 and 90 days on the market, knowing this, if you see a listed property that has been on the market for 300 days, then it's very probable that the owners are more motivated to sell and might be willing to accept a lower offer. A high DOM value is a house flipper's best friend.

Rms: 'Rms' is the most popular abbreviation of the word 'rooms.' The value that accompanies this abbreviation indicates the number of bedrooms inside of the house. If you see a value that is expressed as an addition sum (like '2 + 1'), it probably means that there are two full bedrooms and one potential bedroom (that either needs to be converted or is too small to be considered a full bedroom).

Lot: This refers to the property where the residence is located. The value that accompanies this word is normally the size of the entire property (not just the house) expressed in acres, hectares, or square feet.

Possession: This is a date that is often given in listings that denotes when the seller of property would like to conclude the sale. For most properties, this is as soon as possible, but for some (like those being sold by people moving into retirement communities), it may be listed long before the current owner would like to conclude the sale. As a house flipper, you'll generally only be on the lookout for homes that are immediately available for possession.

Occupation: This is a date that is often given in listings that shows when a seller would be willing to hand over occupation (the right to live in the property) to the buyer. Sometimes you'll find that a listing's occupation date only occurs quite some time after its possession date. This is because some sellers would like to (or need to) live in the property even after it has been sold (this may be because they're waiting for their new home to be built or because they're moving to a different city on a specific date).

Normally if a seller doesn't want to hand over occupation of the property as soon as the sale is concluded, they're liable to pay the new buyer occupational rent for the period that they remain in the house after the deal has been closed. As a house flipper, you generally want to steer clear of any properties whose occupation dates aren't immediately after sale because you ideally want your investment properties to be empty so that you can renovate and rehabilitate them.

Bldg name: This is the most commonly used abbreviation for 'building name.' If the property you're flipping is located in an apartment building or housing complex, its name will be indicated here. It is important to consider the reputation of the building that your potential investment property is located in, as this might affect the maximum selling price that you can ask for it. For example, if it is known to be a crime hotspot, it's likely that you won't be able to ask nearly as much for it as a similar apartment located somewhere safer.

Apx age: This is an abbreviation of the term 'approximate age.' The value that goes along with this abbreviation indicates how old the residence is. As a house flipper, it's important to know the estimated age of a property because it has the potential to affect how much money you'll ultimately be able to ask for it. For example, a historic colonial American home, that was built in the late eighteenth century, is potentially worth a lot more than a similar home that was built more recently. Inversely, a condominium that was built this year is likely to be worth more than a similar one that was built in the 1960s.

Apx sqft: This is an abbreviation of the term 'approximate square feet.' The value that accompanies it is the size of the living space in the residence expressed as square feet. In smaller homes this is normally an exact figure but it may be given as a range in larger homes.

Sqft source: This is an abbreviation of the term 'square foot source' and is used to tell potential buyers how the value given in 'apx sqft' (approximate square feet) was obtained. For example, it might have been taken from the building's architectural plans, blueprint, or floor plan measurements.

Exposure: This term refers to the direction that most of a building's windows face (north, east, south, or west). As a house flipper, you should take note of this information because it affects how favorably potential buyers will view the property. A property will get a lot of light in the morning if it faces east, it will be warmer than west facing houses, but that you'll also need blackout curtains if you plan on sleeping in every morning.

A property will get a lot of sunlight in the afternoon if most of its windows face west, which means that its interior will be set ablaze with a lovely orange glow every evening when the sun sets. It also offers night owls the opportunity to sleep in without the aid of ten thousand drapes or blackout curtains which are often needed to keep bedrooms dark in the early morning hours in east facing houses. A property will be nice, bright, and warm throughout the day if most of its windows face north or south, making north and south the most desirable property exposures. Consequently, you should be the most interested in investing in north and south facing properties.

Pets perm: This is the shortened version of 'pets permitted', and lets you know whether the building in which the residence is located is pet friendly. It's important to take this into account as a house flipper because pet-friendly living spaces tend to be worth more (and thus more worth your while) than living spaces that do not allow pets. Unfortunately, you also need to consider that carpeted, pet-friendly living spaces may need to be re-carpeted during your renovations because some pet owners notoriously neglect to potty train their pets.

Gar/Gar spcs: This is the shortened version of 'garage/garage specifications' and informs the reader whether or not the property has a garage, and if it does, how many cars it can hold. Houses with garage parking for two or more cars tend to be worth exponentially more than properties that do not offer the same amenities. As a house flipper, it's always important to be mindful of the fact that you can convert garage space into living space and vice versa during your renovations.

Unfortunately, simply being able to decipher a property listing is not enough, you also need to learn how to read in between the lines. For example, you can tell a lot about a property by the photographs that are used to advertise it (other than obviously being able to surmise what certain parts of the property look like from them). If a six-bedroom mansion is being advertised, but it's listing only has four photos showing two bedrooms, it's likely that there are some major problems with the house that someone is trying to hide. Luckily, this isn't always a bad thing if you're flipping houses because this might mean that you'll be able to pick up the property for far less than it is inherently worth. You can probably assume much the same thing if most of the photos used in a properties listing show its exterior, as this means that it likely has interior defects that its seller wouldn't like to advertise. Another potential warning sign is if the main exterior photo of the house is taken in portrait instead of in landscape, as this may indicate that the seller is trying to conceal something directly next to the house (like an ugly neighboring home or a construction site). You should also think twice before contacting the seller of a home that's listing photographs have been taken with a wide-angle camera, as these kinds of photos tend to be taken with the intention of purposely misleading potential buyers into thinking that the property is bigger than it actually is.

If you notice that all of the photos used in a property's listing have little orange timestamps and dates in their bottom right-hand corner, you should probably consider making an offer because such a property is likely to be bank-owned as the result of a foreclosure. It will probably be on the market for much less than it is actually worth.

There are also some phrases that listers and sellers often use that actually mean something completely else than what it says on the label. For example, if a property's listing describes it as cute, cozy, darling, or quaint, what the seller actually means is that it's small. If a property's listing describes its amenities or features as 'newer,' you should take this to mean 'not new.' If they had been new, the seller would have said so and there is no definitive agreed-to timeframe for 'newer.' If a seller describes a property as 'needing TLC', what they probably really mean is that you're going to have to set aside quite a bit of money for repairs and renovations.

Fortunately, you don't need to believe everything that a property listing says straight off of the bat, you can check for yourself before you ever physically go to view the place. Making use of some modern magic, you can view the property and its surroundings using software applications like Google Maps or Google Street View. You can even check the potential of the area that the property is located in using WalkScore, which tells you what businesses and amenities are within walking distance of it.

I highly recommend that you don't purchase a property off of its listing alone, and that you personally view it before signing any papers, because listings can be notoriously misleading. You don't want to spend $500,000 on a sprawling mansion that needs some attention, only to find out that it's actually an average-sized home that needs to be demolished, not renovated.

Location, Location, Location

You can't understand house flipping if you don't understand the importance of location to the process. Some areas have incredibly active housing markets that are supported by an increasing demand for residential properties, consequently they're better environments for house flippers, while some areas infamously have housing markets that are experiencing prolonged decreases in demand and consequent decreases in property values, which house flippers should definitely steer clear from.

It's difficult to discuss location on a global scale, so for the sake of simplicity, I'll discuss it on an American one.

Good areas for house flipping are generally easy to spot because they're characterized by a growing formal sector (which in turn leads to a decrease in poverty and unemployment), readily available building materials (which means that they're normally situated near the coast, major highways, railways, or airports), and a possible increase in local tourism (local attractions are often a drawing point).

There are a number of things that make some areas more desirable than others, in for example, they:

- Contain good schools (whose students have been known to get into prestigious colleges and universities)

- Boast of a particularly low crime rate
- Are located somewhere with a particularly nice climate
- Are located close to business or commercial hotspots
- Boast a local college or university
- Are known for their natural beauty
- Are located near the coast or mountains
- Are located in a desirable state or county.

You should make it one of your goals to only flip houses in 'good areas' with growing housing markets because doing so safeguards your investment property from devaluing during your period of ownership of it, which could negatively impact your profit margins.

Some of the best areas for flipping houses in the US are:

- Raleigh, North Carolina
- Denver, Colorado
- Boston, Massachusetts
- Nashville, Tennessee
- Oklahoma City, Oklahoma
- Fort Wayne, Indiana
- Sioux Falls, South Dakota
- El Paso, Texas
- Las Vegas, Nevada
- Phoenix, Arizona
- Orlando, Florida

- Charlotte, North Carolina.

Raleigh has become to house flippers what honey is to flies. It has recently experienced immense growth in its commercial sector, more specifically, it has become somewhat of a mini-silicon valley with all of the tech-companies who have decided to make Raleigh their home. As a result of all of this, more and more people are looking to move to Raleigh. This increase in demand for housing has, as you might expect, strengthened and improved the already existing housing market, and has resulted in two-thirds of all homes being flipped, for an average profit of about 32%. If that isn't the very definition of a 'good area,' then I don't know what is.

Denver is a slightly more expensive area (and was even before house flipping took off, this means that house prices reflect their real value and aren't artificially inflated), and doesn't usually see decent homes being sold for less than $400,000. Of course, this aspect of the area is attractive to house flippers because the increased cost of housing also increases their profit margins.

House flippers also don't have to worry about the housing market in Denver taking a turn for the worst while they're holding on to a flip property because the housing market there is perpetually growing. This is largely due to the fact that Denver is surrounded by mountain ranges which in turn means that the city can't expand any further outwards, meaning that new houses can't be built, which drives up the prices of already existing properties as more and more people are born in and flock to Denver. There has also been an increase in demand for student housing over the past couple of years, which has even made the prospect of flipping much cheaper houses very profitable.

Boston's housing market took a bit of a dip in 2019. However, now is the best possible time to pick up property at a discounted rate there. You can do so with a sound heart because experts believe that the housing market is likely to be revived by some of the urban developments currently taking place in Boston, like the building of a municipal lot and an 'expo' center. Although Boston is a firm favorite among house flippers, it's advisable that you steer clear of investing in 'bargain bin' properties that are unlikely to sell for much, even once they've been renovated, because the inexpensive housing market in Boston isn't nearly as strong as its luxury housing market, which caters to the rich (who are generally more than happy to stretch your profit margin for you).

Nashville is one of America's epicenters of country music, but that's probably not why it's attracting so many house flippers. Its main attraction is the fact that the value of houses in this area increase by about 8% annually. This means that if you bought a house there today for $200,000, you'd be able to sell it in twelve-months for $216,000, even if you didn't make any improvements to it or renovate it at all. The driving force behind its steadily increasing house prices is the fact that more and more employment opportunities become available in this city every single year, more and more housing is needed to give these new employees a place to stay. Nashville's property prices are also quite a bit lower than those in Denver, at an average of $256,000 per home, making it an easier market for beginner investors to access.

If Nashville is still too pricey for you to afford real estate there, you should have a look at Oklahoma City, Oklahoma. Houses here sell for an average price of $128,000, but that doesn't mean that the housing market is stagnating, if anything it's growing every single year. This is mainly due to the fact that this city has become a popular breeding ground for start-up businesses (also largely thanks to its already cheap real estate). This rise in new businesses has rejuvenated the economy, decreasing unemployment rates, and creating a whole host of potential new property owners who you'll likely be able to sell a flipped property to. If you don't want to spend a fortune just to get started, then Oklahoma City might be just the place for you.

Fort Wayne might sound like the name of a settlement straight out of an old black-and-white Western Movie, but it's actually a bustling metropolitan area that has seen a steady increase in housing prices of about 5%, every single year for the past couple of years. This means that if you bought property there for $200,000 right now, it would be worth $210,000 in a year's time, even if you didn't renovate it or make any improvements to it. That sounds like a pretty sweet deal to me. Fort Wayne is still at the beginning of the upswing in its housing prices, now is the best possible time to invest while housing prices are still relatively low (In 2019, an average residential home in Fort Wayne sold for about $120,000.) If you wait too long to jump in, you'll likely find that the median price of a house has increased and that your profit margin has subsequently decreased. The reason for this turnaround in recent years has been that it has become a popular location for first time homeowners, largely due to the fact that the housing market remains so affordable, and that the average cost of living in this area has remained relatively low.

Sioux Falls, South Dakota is another city that has quickly become a favorite among house flippers. Like many of the cities I've already mentioned, it boasts relatively low house prices (with your average family home selling for about $190,000) as well as an annual increase in housing prices. Homes in Sioux Falls increase in value by approximately four percent every twelve months. If you spend $200,000 on a property there right now, then you'd be able to sell it for $208,000 in a year's time even if you didn't make any improvements to it or renovate it. Its low (but steadily increasing) house prices aren't its main attraction though, that honor goes to the incredibly low cost of building and construction materials in the area, which makes renovating houses in Sioux Falls much cheaper than it would be anywhere else.

El Paso offers the same benefits when it comes to building material costs, and its home prices are even lower than those in Sioux Falls, with your average family home selling for just under $130,000. This makes it the ideal city for flippers who are low on cash, and would like to keep all of their costs as low as possible. Labor in this area is also incredibly affordable, making renovations even cheaper than they already are here. Unfortunately, its housing prices have not managed to increase at the same rate as those in other popular house flipping areas, consequently you won't be able to rely on inflation to increase your profit margins for you.

If you have a lot of money to invest in property, then you should consider a more expensive city like Las Vegas, NV. You might need to stretch your wallet a bit in order to be able to afford a home here (with your average family home selling for well over $300,000), but its annual increases in housing prices certainly make it worth it. Vegas homes have steadily been increasing in value by about 12% every year for a while now, this means that if you bought a home there for $300,000, it would be worth about $336,000 within twelve months. That's a lot of growth considering that it's down to nothing but inflation. This spectacular annual increase has drawn hordes of house flippers to Vegas, so it's no surprise that nearly a third of all houses bought or sold here are done so as part of a flip. On top of the serious advantage that inflation offers house flippers, most of them have also been able to make nearly 30% in profit on every flip. Vegas is a house flipper's heaven, so it's a pity that it's nothing but a pipe dream to so many.

There aren't many popular house flipping cities that are more expensive than Las Vegas is, but that doesn't mean that they don't exist. Phoenix, Arizona is one of them. Your average family home sells for well over $320,000 in this city, but that hasn't stopped it for becoming a house flipping mecca. Phoenix sees more houses being flipped every year than any other city in North America. Its popularity is somewhat surprising when you consider that it doesn't offer the annual increase in average house prices that many other areas offer. Its only draw is the more than 35% difference it offers flippers on the price that they buy an investment property for, compared to the price that they're able to sell it for.

If you like Disneyland, then you'll love Orlando. Although your average family home in this city sells for well over $250,000, its outskirts are filled with older homes in the $100,000 price ranges that just need a little love to compete with those in the $250,000 price range. While Orlando's city center has steadily been growing, many of the suburbs surrounding it have fallen into disrepair because of their aging populations. Luckily, this makes Orlando an affordable investment despite its proximity to Mickey Mouse's house. Unfortunately, Disney's magic hasn't breathed any life into Orlando's housing market. You won't be able to rely on the annual increase in housing prices that other areas offer, but that doesn't mean that all is lost. You can expect to be able to sell an investment property in this city for 40% more than the price you originally paid for it after renovations, this means that you can expect to sell a home that you bought for $200,000 for about $280,000.

If you're looking to invest in an affluent city that's more off of the beaten track than Orlando or Vegas, you should consider buying property in Charlotte, North Carolina. Like many other affluent areas, it doesn't offer the same annual increase in housing prices that many cheaper areas do, but you can expect to make about 20% profit on every single property that you flip here (especially if you stick to older, more dilapidated homes in or on the outskirts of already popular areas). Charlotte is expected to experience a rapid boom in commerce over the next couple of years, this means that although there's not currently enough demand to drive up house prices annually, there might well be in the future.

Of course, while there are cities that are ideal for house flipping, there are also cities in which flips are almost always doomed from the start. Ten of these infamous cities are:

- Bridgeport, Connecticut
- Yonkers, New York
- Newark, New Jersey
- Oakland, California
- San Francisco, California
- Wilmington, Delaware
- Boston, Massachusetts
- New Haven, Connecticut
- New York, New York
- Los Angeles, California.

These cities all have different reasons for their house flipping failure rate, but it essentially boils down to the fact that properties there have either already peaked in value (this means that renovating them doesn't add much value, as is the case in New York), or they're so low in value and demand that finding a buyer for them once they've been renovated is nearly impossible. You should avoid cities where unemployment rates are high, where renting is preferred to homeownership, where the price of living is high in relation to the average citizen's earnings, and where houses spend more than 100 days, on average, on the market before being sold.

How to Choose an Investment Property

Once you've made up your mind that you want to improve your financial position forever by getting involved in the real estate market, it's time to choose your very first investment property.

Before you run off and start scouring real estate websites or hounding sellers, you might want to consider getting pre-approved for a mortgage. Getting pre-approval for this kind of loan essentially means that you get a letter from the bank or lending institution that says that they're willing to loan you an amount of money up to a certain specified amount. Having pre-approval puts you in a better bargaining position, and makes the seller more likely to accept any offers that you might make because they'll be guaranteed that you're in the position to pay the offered amount. I highly recommend that you look into getting pre-approval before you start shopping around, not only because it will make buying property easier, but also because it will give you a better idea of whether your pre-planned budget is realistic or not.

The first step of getting preapproval for a mortgage involves checking your credit score. Your credit score is a number between 300 and 850, that financial institutions like banks and lending companies use in order to gauge your creditworthiness. It is based on how well you've been able to meet your financial obligations in the past, and details the number of credit agreements that you've been a party to. If you've entered numerous credit agreements in the past, and paid them all on time, you should have a relatively high credit score. However, if you've never taken on any debt before, or if you've been late on a number of payments to creditors, then it's likely that your credit score will be rather low.

In most cases, you'll need a credit score of at least 620 in order to receive pre-approval, although you should contact the lending institution that you have in mind to inquire about their requirements. Luckily, it is relatively easy to check your credit score. You can check it for free once every twelve months on annualcreditreport.com, a website that compiles reports from TransUnion, Equifax, and Experian.

Once you've checked your credit score and looked to see whether it meets the minimum requirements of the financial institution that you have in mind, you should start collecting all of the documents that you need to be able to apply for a mortgage pre-approval. Normally these documents are proof of income, proof of your social security number, your investment account details, proof of your address (like a utility bill in your name), and your employment details.

If you're an aspiring house flipper, it's a good idea to avoid jumping around from job to job with long periods of unemployment in between because financial institutions generally only issue mortgage pre-approvals to applicants who have been continuously employed for a 24-month period. This is because lenders want to see proof that you'll be employed during the loan period, and thus that you'll be able to make the required payments every month. The only real exception to this rule is if you're self-employed. Although self-employment doesn't disqualify you from getting pre-approval, you generally need to be able to prove that you've been making money while being self-employed for at least two years (as a result of this you can't simply label yourself 'self-employed' to dodge having to provide proof of income).

You can approach lending institutions and start applying for pre-approval as soon as you have all of the required documents at your disposal. It's best to shop around a little by applying to a number of lenders and seeing who offers you the highest pre-approval with the best interest rates. It's never a good idea to only apply to one lender or to go with the first pre-approval that you get because it's always possible that you could have gotten a better deal elsewhere, and successfully flipping houses is all about saving money wherever possible.

Pre-approval in hand, you'll be ready to start viewing properties and potentially making offers, but how do you know whether you'll be able to make money reselling a property? The truth is that there are a number of factors to consider, but there is a lot you can do to make sure that your chances of reselling a property for a sizable profit are high.

We discussed popular house flipping cities in chapter one, but there's more to location than just what the road signs near your property say. Some aspects of your property's location might decrease its value in the eyes of potential buyers, while some aspects of your property's location might have the opposite effect, making them more desirable to buyers and thus increasing their value. Ideally you want to try to invest in houses that are situated in good neighborhoods with low crime rates, and that are located near well-performing schools, beautiful parks, accessible biking or hiking trails, theaters or cinemas, malls, the coast, the mountains, or commercial city centers. You want to try to avoid properties that are situated on busy streets, within sight of or within hearing distance of busy highways, near airports or railways, or that are in untidy, poor, or unsightly neighborhoods with high crime rates. The rule of thumb is that if you wouldn't want to live there, you shouldn't buy a house to flip there.

You need more than just a good neighborhood to get ahead though, ideally your prospective property should be 'good' within its neighborhood too. What I mean by that is that it would be pointless to acquire a mobile home situated on a large lot in between a number of huge Tuscan-style villas. In this case, the neighborhood might be good but your property looks so poor in comparison to its neighbors that no potential buyer would ever consider it. However, if you owned a mobile home situated on a large lot in a trailer park where the other lots were half the size, then it would seem like an attractive option to potential buyers, and you'd likely have no trouble selling it. You want to make sure that your investment property is of the same quality as those around it, although ideally it should be even better, as this will make it easier to sell.

Perhaps a more realistic example of this principle at work is if you were looking to buy a property in a neighborhood where all of the houses are 1,400 square foot in size with a single garage and a pool. An investment home in this neighborhood that is 1,200 in size with a single garage and no pool would be a bad idea, but if you found a home there that was 1,600 in size with a double garage and a pool, you should buy it immediately because it would be a fantastic investment.

Surveys have found that buyers are more likely to be interested in properties that are situated on lots that are larger than those belonging to the neighbors. Houses that are more 'private' (further away from neighbors and with fencing or walls to keep out any unwanted visitors) also tend to sell much faster. The National Association of Home Builders conducted a study a couple of years ago, in an attempt to better understand what motivates buyers to buy any specific home, and their findings are rather interesting.

They found that nine-tenths of all potential buyers wouldn't consider purchasing a house without a laundry room, that the same number also eliminated houses without energy-reducing windows and most, ideally, wanted a patio. Also, just over 80% of all potential buyers indicated that they really wanted ceiling fans, garage storage, exterior lighting, hardwood flooring, and a double kitchen sink. Another study that is titled *2019 Remodeling Impact Report* found that buyers were the most keen to buy homes that had recently had their heating, ventilation, and air conditioning (HVAC) systems replaced or their kitchens renovated or upgraded.

The same studies also noted a couple of key things that seem to put buyers off. They found that some of the most common deterrents are carpeting all throughout the house (buyers seem to prefer tiled, masonry, or wooden floors), a closed-plan layout, or a garden that will need a lot of maintenance if you want to keep it in its current condition. Some house flippers also make the mistake of including media rooms, trophy rooms, game rooms, or home offices in their newly renovated investment properties, which is unfortunate because survey respondents seem to indicate that these kinds of rooms are rather undesirable.

Other than excluding properties based on their location or physical attributes, you should also exclude all of those built during or before 1978. No, it's not to avoid hauntings, rather it's to avoid the terror that is lead paint. Before 1978, homeowners regularly used to paint their living areas, bathrooms, kitchens, and bedrooms with lead paint. Lead paint was incredibly vibrant in color, which originally made it every interior decorators dream, but the beginning of the 1970s saw increasing evidence that exposing young children to lead paint could lead to brain damage, toxicity, kidney damage, and nerve damage. Not only is lead nasty stuff but the Environmental Protection Agency (EPA) has also made it illegal to disturb any wall (interior or exterior) that has been painted with lead paint unless you have been certified by them. Certification can cost more than 500 dollars depending on where you are located and consists of attending a short course on the proper procedure to be followed pertaining to lead paint.

However, there is a loophole. If you can manage to flip the house without painting over or otherwise disturbing any of the lead paint, your liability only stretches as far as having to inform potential buyers of the presence of the lead paint and handing them an EPA pamphlet titled '*Protect Your Family From Lead In Your Home.*' If you don't abide by the EPA's rules regarding selling homes containing lead paint, you may be fined up to $30,000 (an expense most house flippers certainly can't afford). The easiest way to avoid the entire lead paint rigmarole is by avoiding houses that are older than 42 years old entirely (they're less popular with buyers anyway).

You should also steer clear of properties that need extensive repairs or renovations in order to be resellable (especially as a beginner house flipper). Needing to do too many repairs can turn a quick flip into a lengthy renovation, decreasing your profit margin by every day that the property's sale is delayed. Ideally you want to focus on properties that only need a couple of aesthetic adjustments before you'll be able to sell them for a profit. Properties that you should avoid like the plague are those with structural issues like foundation cracks, sagging floors, uneven floors, a sinking foundation, or major roof leaks. The problem with structural defects is that they're expensive to rectify and you'll probably need a construction expert's help in order to fix them (which in and of itself comes at a premium). The golden rule of house flipping is to keep your costs as low as possible, which obviously takes major repairs off of the cards. The problem with structural defects is that they can be hard to spot, and unless the seller knows about them, you can't hold them liable for the cost of repairs after the sale has been concluded. Consequently, one of the main tasks facing aspiring house flippers is learning how to spot structural problems at a distance.

One of the main causes of structural damage to homes in the US is termites. Governmental studies indicate that termite damage costs American homeowners more than $5 billion annually, an infestation has the potential to do a lot of financial damage (and infestations are more common than one might think). Termites slowly eat away at the wooden frames of houses, putting their structural integrity at risk as the infestation grows and continues to do further damage. You should avoid investing in properties with termite infestations at all costs.

Fortunately, there are some things that you can look out for when viewing a potential investment property that are indicative of a termite infestation, these are droppings that resemble pellets made out of sawdust or coffee grounds found near wooden structures or surfaces, little tubes of mud on the exterior of the house (these are the entrances that termites use to gain access to a house), discarded wings lying around near doors or windows (termites grow wings to fly to new colonies), hollowed-out wooden structures or slabs, and wooden floors that are lifting or that have blisters in them (as termites like to nest under wooden floors, causing them to become distorted).

Roof leaks are another defect to keep an eye out for. While roof leaks themselves count as structural damage, they can be a sign of an even bigger underlying problem that could require more than just a little patching here and there to fix. They can also be a sign that the roof's cladding has reached the natural end of its three decade long life span or that the house's frame has dangerously shifted (perhaps due to a faulty foundation or earthquake damage). All in all, it's normally not worth it to invest in a property with a history of having a leaky roof, it's best to just avoid them entirely.

If you spot any ceiling or wall cracks in a property during your initial viewing, you should also reconsider investing in it because they could be indicative of the fact that the property's structural integrity is no longer intact. The most dangerous cracks of all are those located directly above doorways or those that are found on the ceiling that are accompanied by discoloration or sagging. Cracks in the walls can also be a sign that a property's foundation has sagged or shifted, a problem that could take tens of thousands of dollars to correct.

If you notice that a potential investment property's floors are uneven, you should hesitate before putting any money down on it. Uneven floors are often caused by damage to the sub-floor supports. Investing in a property that has this type of damage, might mean having to replace floors or having to re-stump the floor entirely (both of which are expensive activities to undertake). You'll be able to find a home with a level floor, trust me, so there's absolutely no good reason to take the risk of buying a home that confuses a laser level.

Another good rule of thumb is to avoid houses with damp basements. If you notice that a property's basement smells moldy or is particularly moist while viewing it, you should probably thank the owner and walk away as quickly as possible. Damp subfloors are the result of insufficient ventilation, and not only do they smell like a 1,000-year-old forest's floor, but they're dangerous as well, because they're incredibly hospitable to the growth of fungus and mold which, in turn, can rot away the structure of the house from the bottom up. Some kinds of mold, like black mold, are also potentially hazardous to your health.

You should also strike any properties with crumbling concrete structures off your 'maybe' list. Concrete only crumbles when it is exposed to moisture, this means that it's indicative of a larger problem with dampness that could originate from the roof or the house's plumbing. Roof and plumbing problems are almost always pricey to rectify, so it's logical to avoid properties that show signs of having them.

If you can peek through a gap between a house's exterior wall and one of its interior walls, it's not the house for you (no matter how gorgeous it might be otherwise). This phenomenon generally only occurs if there's a problem with the house's foundation, or if its support pillars have been incorrectly erected or damaged by dampness or termites. It's never a good omen, and while the peepholes might be fun in the beginning, houses with this problem are usually not good investments.

Some of the most significant signs of structural damage are often the most overlooked, doors and windows that won't open or close properly are probably the best example of this. If you're viewing a house and notice that its doors or windows seem to be or get 'stuck,' you might be tempted to think that it's likely just down to sloppy installation, but the truth is that it can be a sign of much bigger problems. Windows and doors that won't open or close can be symptoms of movement under the house itself, which could be because of problems with the stumps the house is resting on or the concrete slab that makes up its foundation (depending on the build of the house).

Once you've found the house that you want to invest in, you should apply the '70% rule' to it to see if it is likely to be a profitable flip, before making an offer on it. The 70% rule is a well-known rule of thumb in the house flipping community. It essentially states that you should absolutely never buy a house for more than 70% of what it will be worth by the time that you decide to sell it.

For example, if you were looking to buy a 1,400 square foot property with three bedrooms in El Paso that would be worth $200,000 after renovations, you should avoid paying more than $140,000 for it. This rule is incredibly nifty because it helps you to figure out how much you could offer for a property while still being able to make a profit from flipping it. If you buy a property for more than 70% of its after repair value, then it is incredibly likely that you'll either break even or suffer a loss once it's sold.

It's important to view at least ten properties before buying your first property to flip. First time flippers are prone to falling in love with the first property that they view, and buying it basically on first sight, but this isn't the proper way to approach your new venture. If you don't view a number of properties, you won't get an accurate idea of what you can get for your money, this means that you might end up buying a mediocre house for $300,000 when you could have purchased an amazing home for $250,000.

I recommend that you have an idea of the kind of property that you'd like to buy before you start house hunting, simply because the number of properties for sale out there can be overwhelming and having a clear idea of the house you'd like to buy can help you to keep on track to fulfilling that vision.

How to Renovate Your Investment Property

Many house flippers have dubbed renovating their favorite part of the process, and it's easy to understand why. This part of the process allows you to harness your creative energies in an attempt to create, not only your potential buyers' dream home, but the home you've been dreaming of too. While it's important to make the kind of changes that you'd like to see made in a property, it's more important to be mindful of the kind of changes that will increase the value of the property and attract potential buyers.

The first step is to take a look at the other houses in your investment property's neighborhood. This will give you a good idea of the improvements that you need to make in order to bring your investment property up to par with the rest of the homes in the area. For example, if all of your property's neighbors have swimming pools, you should strongly consider having a swimming pool installed to make your home just as attractive to buyers as other homes for sale in the neighborhood are.

The second step is to ensure that the house looks appealing from the street. First impressions matter, and if you don't make a good one with potential buyers, they might subconsciously decide not to buy your property before even having the chance to view its interior. Scientists agree that first impressions are normally created within seven seconds. This means that you have seven seconds from the time that potential buyers first lay eyes on your property to wow them. There are a few simple things that you can do to improve how your property looks from the street, but your go-to improvements should be to keep the lawn trimmed (and green), to trim and shape any hedges or bushes, to replace the mailbox, to add some shutters to the property's street-facing windows, to repaint the front door a quirky color (perhaps to match the shutters you've just added), to install some outdoor lighting, to plant some flowers that are colorful and in bloom, and to replace the front door's doorknob. You might also want to consider repainting the exterior of the house if its current paint job has started cracking or flaking off. Nobody wants to live in a scaly house.

The third step is to upgrade the property's bathrooms and kitchen. The extensiveness of your upgrades will depend on how much money you can justify spending on them while still maintaining a reasonable profit margin, although a survey conducted by US News found that you should expect to spend about $10,000 to entirely revamp a single bathroom, and about $16,000 to entirely revamp a kitchen.

This might sound overly pricey but it's important to remember that bathrooms and kitchens rank high on buyers' priority lists, so putting some extra effort into them generally pays off. If at all possible, you should consider having a standing shower with amenities like a bench and a massage shower head installed as buyers have consistently ranked this feature very high when quizzed on features that are likely to sway them to buy a property. You should also ensure that the kitchen cabinets are in good condition (and replace them if they're not). Ideally you would also paint them a light color like white or beige as this is currently the most fashionable color in kitchen design.

You might be tempted to turn your first investment property into the kind of property that you'd like to live in yourself, but it's important to keep in mind that you need to make it attractive to the highest number of potential buyers as is practically possible. This means avoiding giving it too much of your 'personal touch.' Rather, you should try to make sure that its color scheme and furnishings are as neutral as possible and that you remove any personal effects like family photos, children's toys, and decorative trinkets before offering any viewings.

Polls indicate that some of the most common features that are likely to put off potential buyers are interior or exterior walls that are painted unusual colors (like black, dark blue, pink, purple, green, or red), unusual flooring (like funky carpets from the 1960s, shaggy rugs, colorful tiles, or unconventional flooring materials like bare concrete), cheap or tacky faucets or faucet handles (like those fake crystal faucet handles your grandma's house probably had), walls covered in wood paneling or wallpaper (no matter how stylish you may that they are), brass or brass-colored fixtures, kitchen appliances that don't match each other (for example, if your oven is stainless steel, your dishwasher should be stainless steel too), acoustic tile ceilings, popcorn-finished ceilings, and dropped ceilings. Essentially, you want to try to make your investment property look like a home straight out of *House & Garden* magazine instead of using it as a canvas for your own artistic preferences.

The most important thing to consider when you're thinking about renovating an investment property is cost. You might be willing to take the risk of committing to major improvements and renovations, but sometimes doing so is simply illogical from a business point of view. For example, potential buyers would probably love a $20,000 walk-in hot tub-style bath tub, but it wouldn't be practical to invest in one for a home that you won't be able to sell for more than $200,000 anyway. Big improvements and renovations only make sense if it's a very expensive property, or if your profit margin was huge to start off with, otherwise making them is just a way of robbing yourself of profit.

You might also want to consider making a couple of landscaping upgrades, and while this isn't a bad idea, there are some common mistakes that many first time house flippers make that you should try to avoid. The most prolific of which is having a pool installed. It's not always a bad idea to install a pool as long as all of the other houses in the neighborhood have one too, but if none (or very few) of the neighbors have one, then you should probably give this home improvement a skip. Installing a pool can be an expensive endeavor (and you should expect to spend about $30,000 to have it done properly). Not only will having it done cost you a pretty penny but pools have actually been known to drive away potential buyers. The reasons for this are numerous but the main ones are that pools are both expensive and time-consuming to maintain, and they're a hazard to families with young children who might be in danger of drowning.

Landscaping endeavors that you definitely should undertake are removing any dead or unsightly plants, planting grass, or having a new lawn installed where it has previously turned brown or died, putting away any features that might make the garden space look smaller than it actually is (like above ground trampolines, volleyball nets, and soccer goalposts), planting new plants where the garden looks a bit bare, keeping the existing lawn trimmed until the property is sold, and raking up any unsightly or seasonal leaves. Additionally, you should also consider power-washing any walkways, pathways, or driveways that the property might have before offering it up for viewings.

At the end of the day, the extensiveness of your renovations will have to be decided by your own discretion. Before embarking on any improvements, you should seriously consider whether the improvements you want to make will increase the value of your investment property. There's no point in making improvements that won't equate to a bigger return on investment for you (unless you like doing hard work for free). Some house flippers believe that you should make as few material improvements to a property as possible while others argue that making a few carefully considered improvements is worth it in the long run. Where you'll fall on this spectrum depends entirely on your methodology and the strategy you'd ultimately like to follow.

Chapter 3:

What not to Do

By now, you should be pretty clued-up on what you need to do to make a success out of flipping houses, you may even have gone as far as memorizing some of the golden rules that I have mentioned, but if you really want to make millions (or even billions) by flipping houses you also need to know what not to do.

Normally you'd only be able to learn what not to do by getting started, making a million mistakes, and trying not to repeat them again, but the wonders of modern science have made it possible for us to predict which courses of action are likely to result in failure without you having to learn to spot them through trial and error.

There are five common mistakes that have cost thousands of house flippers tons of money: not having enough initial capital to start off with, incorrectly calculating your expenses or costs, neglecting to obtain the required building permits, not getting property insurance, and incorrectly pricing your property for sale.

Not Having Enough Start-Up Capital

If you've picked up this book, you probably want to start your house flipping career as soon as possible, and who can blame you? Nobody wants to wait to become a millionaire, life's far too short for that. Here's the thing though, sometimes it's better to wait until you have a little bit more capital to inject into a property before getting started.

There are a couple of good reasons to wait until you have enough capital saved up to make a substantial investment. Firstly, if you go into a flipping project while you're strapped for cash, you are going to struggle to effect the kind of changes and renovations that are likely to add a substantial amount of value to a property. If you don't have enough money to redo a bathroom, for example, you're essentially just wasting your time picking up an investment property because your profits (if any) will be minimal.

Secondly, if you invest in properties that are the cheapest ones that you can get your hands on, it's unlikely that you'll be able to increase their value by much, even if you do commit to undertaking major renovations and repairs. Properties that fall into this price class are often inexpensive for more reasons than just their aesthetic appeal, they're also usually located in undesirable or unsafe neighborhoods, or they're otherwise unsuitable for your average buyer for whatever reason. For example, you might be able to buy a shack that's falling apart in the middle of nowhere for $50,000, but even if you install a gold-plated toilet in it, you won't be able to resell it for more than $55,000.

Struggling to come up with enough initial capital to make a worthwhile investment is a common obstacle that many aspiring house flippers face. Luckily, there are a couple of ways to tackle this hurdle. To start off, it's important to realize that your first couple of flips might not be extremely profitable or the kind of projects that you ultimately want to end up working on. It's crucial not to become demotivated because of this, no matter how disheartening it may be, it's an entirely normal and expected start. One of the most straightforward ways to build up your investment capital is to start flipping properties with small profit margins until you've saved up enough to make a more substantial investment. For example, even if you only make $5,000 in profit on your first two or three flips, you shouldn't see this as a failure, but as an opportunity to save $10,000 or $15,000 to put towards your next project. In this way, you'll be able to slowly increase the value of the properties that you're dealing in overtime.

Putting your initial profits back into your planned investment capital is just one way of ensuring that you'll consistently be able to afford better and better properties. Another popular way of increasing your investment capital is as old as time (and real estate) itself: saving up your own personal income to increase your spending power. Admittedly, this option takes a bit longer than just reinjecting your initial profits back into your budget, but that doesn't mean that it's entirely impractical or useless.

The easiest ways to save money are also the most well-known: take public transport instead of investing in a car or driving, cook at home instead of eating out, resist the urge to update your wardrobe, cut down on luxuries like holidays and entertainment, and cancel any unused or unnecessary subscriptions. If you've implemented all of the traditional money saving mechanisms, but you're still not happy with the amount that you're managing to squirrel away every month, you might want to consider making use of some less conventional saving mechanisms. Personally, I'd recommend making use of 'apps' like Digit, Clarity Money, Qapital, Acorns, You Need A Budget, and Honey.

We're living in the computer age, so why shouldn't you make use of the magic of technology to optimize your finances? Digit is absolutely free to use for the first 100 days, so I recommend that you download it immediately. This application tracks your income and expenses, and then uses a complex algorithm to calculate how much money you can afford to put aside every month without having to live like a leper. Not only does it do all of the *yucky* math for you, but it actually goes ahead and subtracts the calculated amount from your account and deposits it into a savings account on your behalf.

With Digit, you hardly even have to be involved in your finances, and you can still remain fiscally responsible despite being somewhat absent otherwise. You might not save enough using this platform to make a down payment on a house within a fortnight, but your savings will definitely add up over a couple of months, potentially affording you the ability to afford a property in a higher price bracket.

Clarity Money won't manage your savings account for you, but it can be used to save money on your set monthly payments. It does this by contacting the companies and departments that bill you every month and negotiating with them to see if it can't secure a lower repayment or interest rate for you. The money that you can save every month due to your reduced payments, can go a long way to improving your position as a house flipper, so it's definitely not something to scoff at.

On top of renegotiating your bills and payments, Clarity Money also goes through all of your subscribed payments and cancels those that you no longer use or don't need. You might be surprised to find out how many unnecessary payments you're making to companies you don't even know every month, which is exactly why this application is worth its weight in gold (metaphorically speaking, of course).

Qapital is another wonderful financial application that deposits money straight into your savings account, plumping it up in the blink of an eye. It does this by rounding up every single purchase that you make to the nearest dollar and depositing the difference between this sum and the actual purchase price into an approved savings account on your behalf. For example, if you purchased a burger for $3.10, it would round up the transaction to $4, and deposit the remaining $0.90 into your savings account.

This might not sound like a significant amount of money but over time all of those small savings really add up. When used in conjunction with one of the previously discussed financial applications, Qapital can help you to raise a substantial amount of capital over the course of a couple of months. Saving money is all about discipline, but Qapital makes saving money a painless experience, you probably won't even notice the difference in your finances (although you'll definitely notice the difference in your savings).

Acorns is like Qapital on steroids. Just like Qapital, it rounds up your purchases to the nearest dollar, but unlike Qapital it doesn't simply stuff these savings into a low earning savings account, it actually invests them in the stock market on your behalf with the intention of exponentially increasing them through careful trading.

It manages to do this successfully by investing your spare cents in exchange traded funds (ETFs).

ETFs are much more predictable than individual stocks are, so it's unlikely that Acorns will lose any of your money by investing it on your behalf. Acorns is generally a good fit for most house flippers because it allows you to feel that your savings are being made to work for you, instead of it having to be the other way around. Imagine how much extra money you could pocket every month if you used this application in conjunction with Clarity Money.

You Need A Budget is an application that does exactly what it says on the label. It tracks and makes note of all or your income and expenses, and uses this information to draw up a budget for you. Not only will it create a personalized wealth improvement program that you can use to plan your finances, but it will also explain to you why your ideal budget looks the way that it looks.

You Need A Budget's goal is to teach you how to budget, so instead of simply spoon-feeding you financial plans, it offers you the opportunity to learn more about how to prioritize and optimize your own income and expenses. This application is ready to teach you everything high school failed to tell you about managing your money.

Honey is as sweet as its name suggests it to be. Downloading this application will give you instant access to hundreds of thousands of coupons and discount codes worldwide. Not only does Honey notify you of these coupons and discount codes, but it actually goes ahead and applies them to any online purchases that you may make. This application essentially gives you the opportunity to buy everything imaginable for just that little bit cheaper. One discounted item certainly won't pay for a bathroom's renovations, but one or two hundred discounted items could definitely put you well on your way to installing whatever ridiculous bathroom accessories that you were envisioning.

If saving, traditionally or digitally, just isn't your thing, and you don't want to spend money flipping houses for smaller profits to be able to afford one decent investment property, then you might want to consider liquidating some of your assets in order to raise some initial investment capital. Many house flippers sell one of their family cars in order to be able to afford their first proper flip, although realistically you could also pawn jewelry, collectors' items, art, furniture, or even clothes to raise money for a down payment. It might sound a bit depressing (if not downright humiliating) to part with your personal effects to be able to finance your new venture, but it's important to remember that you'll earn back the value of the items you sacrifice, ten-fold, once your house flipping career is in full swing.

When push comes to shove, you have a number of tools at your disposal to help you to improve your profit margin by allowing you to save up more money to spend on flipping houses. The most difficult part of saving is finding the method that works best for you, so it's fortunate that this chapter should serve as a relatively helpful guide to help you find the most suitable technique for you.

Incorrectly Calculating Your Expenses and Costs

Incorrectly calculating expenses and costs, has probably historically cost house flippers more money than termites have (and that's saying something). It's easy to fool yourself into thinking that you are spending much less money on an investment property than you actually are, and while optimism is generally considered a positive personality trait, it's something that you should try to avoid in business. The reason why underestimating your expenses and costs is so problematic is that you'll be unable to calculate your required minimum selling price. If you aren't honest with yourself, you won't be able to estimate how much money you'll need to spend on the property before you're able to sell it for a profit.

Many house flippers regularly underestimate the cost of renovations, especially if they're largely tackling them as do-it-yourself projects, but this isn't actually the snare that seems to cut short so many house flippers' love for real estate. That honor would go to forgetting to take utility costs, rates, and taxes into account. It's incredibly easy to forget that you'll likely be holding on to your investment property for two or three months (at the least) before you're able to sell it. During this time period, you might have to pay property taxes or levies, and you'll certainly have to pay for waste removal and electricity. If you're making use of a lot of electrical power tools in order to do renovations, you may be unpleasantly surprised to find quite a substantial electricity bill waiting for you at the end of the month.

Miscalculating your expenses by a couple of hundred dollars might not seem like a big deal if you're expecting to make $60,000 in profit on a flip. But it's likely that, if you've missed a couple of dollars here and there that you know of, then you've actually missed a myriad of expenses that you're not even aware of. Even if you haven't, a bunch of small miscalculations can really add up in the long run.

For example, if renovating the bathroom cost you $1,500 more than you expected, if you forgot to calculate in a $300 electricity bill, if you ended up spending an unexpected $500 on cleaning materials like carpet shampoos or disinfectants, and if you neglect to consider the $1,500 you owe the landscaping company, you'd end up making a profit that is nearly $4,000 less than you initially anticipated. That's quite a difference, and not only would going through a calculation blunder like this be quite disheartening, but it could also seriously damage your financial position too.

There's no quick fix or 'app' that can help you to avoid miscalculating your expenses and costs. Unfortunately, the only surefire way to avoid this pitfall is by sitting down and drawing up a carefully considered table containing all of your expenditures, and going through it as thoroughly as Santa examines his naughty and nice lists (because, as we all know, he checks them twice). It might even be wise to ask an independent third party to check your expenses list for you as a fresh pair of eyes might help you to spot some costs that you may have previously missed.

Incorrectly Pricing Your Property

One of the easiest ways to shrink your profit margins is to have your investment property remain 'on the market' for too long. If it takes you months and months to sell your first flipping property, you'll rack up taxes, levies, and utilities bills at disproportionate rates, all of which will eat away at the difference between the money you had to spend on the property, and how much you'll be able to sell it for. The leading cause of homes remaining on the market for increased periods of time is properties that are incorrectly priced, or rather properties that have been put up for sale for a sum of money that is far more than they're actually worth to potential buyers.

Fortunately, this shouldn't be a problem if you're making use of the services of a real estate agent. Real estate agents are trained, and often have years and years of experience, in correctly valuing and pricing homes and investment properties. If a well-respected real estate agent tells you that your investment property is currently worth *X*-amount, you probably shouldn't expect to be able to sell it for much more than that.

The problem comes in when you choose not to make use of a real estate agent's services, and are left to your own devices to determine your property's worth. Of course, that's not to say that it's entirely impossible for a layman to correctly estimate a house's value, but there is an inherent degree of difficulty to it simply because you generally need to have a very holistic oversight of the property market in order to be able to accurately do so. And as a beginner house flipper, it's unlikely that you'll have that kind of experience to aid you.

So, how do you go about estimating your investment property's sale price when you're entirely new to the game? Well, the easiest way is to look at property listings belonging to similar properties in the same area. For example, if you are trying to figure out how much your 3-bedroom, 2-bathroom property, in an up-and-coming part of Houston, Texas is worth, you'd need to look at the advertisements of other 3-bedroom, 2-bathroom properties in the same area. If they're all worth $300,000, the chances are pretty good that that's what your property is worth too.

Of course, if your 3-bedroom, 2-bathroom property is objectively better than the properties whose listings you have studied, it's likely worth $20,000 or $30,000 more. Inversely, if it's not up to the same standard as the other properties whose listings you have reviewed, your property may be worth a couple of thousand dollars less. Unfortunately there's no hard and fast rule to use when it comes to calculating your investment property's worth, instead it boils down to a good dose of logic and careful consideration.

Chapter 4:

Assess Your Character

You're probably wondering why there's a chapter on character and personality in a business and finance book. After all, you've come here for the nitty-gritty stuff, not the airy-fairy stuff. Alas, you'd be entirely mistaken to think that who you are as a person, has no effect on your success as a house flipper. Not only does your character and personality determine how likely you are to make a success of flipping houses, it can also help you to determine which flipping strategy you should use.

Why Your Personality Matters

According to some researchers, the likelihood of you being successful, as an entrepreneur or business-person, can be divined by looking at your Myers-Briggs personality profile. Myers-Briggs personality profiles are derived from a self-test that can be performed to gain insight into how a person perceives themselves, the world, and the people around them. These scientists have found that people whose results indicate that they're ESTP, ENTJ, or INTJ personality types, are more likely to make it into the top one percent (or the upper middle class, at the very least).

People who are classified as belonging to the ESTP personality type are social butterflies, made easily identifiable by their love for spending time around people and their general lack of social anxiety. On the other hand, people who the test identified as belonging to the ENTJ group, are stereotypically over-achievers who also tend to be prone to over-competitiveness. The third most financially successful group, the INTJ personality type, are thinkers. Albert Einstein himself would have belonged to the INTJ group, a category that is characterized by quiet individuals with deep thoughts. If any of these sound like you, it's entirely possible that you were born with an inherent financial advantage encoded into your character (thanks mom and dad).

Of course, Myers-Briggs aren't the only psychological tests that have been employed to try to determine individuals' suitability as business owners and entrepreneurs. Decades ago, two heart specialists, Ray Rosenman and Meyer Friedman, theorized that all people could be categorized into one of two personality groups: type-A personalities and type-B personalities.

While they unfortunately found that type-A personalities were more likely to develop heart disease, they also found that people with type-A personalities were more likely to make it big in the world of business. If you would describe yourself as being an ambitious overachiever who is competitive, outgoing, proactive, and organized, then you're a type-A personality, which means that you should start investing in real estate immediately because you're likely to make a fortune doing it.

Don't despair if none of these personality types sound like you. The entire reason why I'm emphasizing the importance of familiarizing yourself with your character traits is because once you know them, you can start working on changing them if they're not conducive to helping you to achieve your goals. A personality test might reveal that you're naturally introverted, and in a world where extroversion is the currency of kings, this is somewhat problematic. However, knowing that you're prone to introversion can help you to strive to be (or at least pretend to be) a bit more confident and outgoing in your business dealings. That's the purpose of understanding your personality, giving yourself the opportunity to transform into the kind of person who becomes a real estate mogul.

Getting to Know Yourself

But how do you go about getting to know yourself? It can be difficult to be honest with yourself about who you really are. We're rarely the people we imagine ourselves to be, for better or for worse. The easiest, but by far the least pleasant, way to gain insight into your character is to ask your friends and family how they experience you. You're likely to get an accurate idea of your personality profile from them, although the likelihood of a bruised ego is high too.

If, like most of us, you're not brave enough to follow the aforementioned approach, you might want to consider making use of one of the hundreds of reliable free personality tests that are out there. They're always great to share on Facebook, but you can also use them to check if your personality traits match those that are commonly shared by successful real estate investors. If you're interested in finding out what your Myers-Briggs personality type is, you might want to consider heading over to 16personalities.com.

This website gives you the opportunity to find out whether you have one of three most entrepreneurially successful personality types out there, and the test only takes about 12 minutes to complete. You don't have to set aside a significant portion of your day to take it. To top it all off, getting your Myers-Briggs results on this website is free, it's the money-smart thing to do.

Persona Bubble is another fantastic option, and even allows you to compare your results to those of other people in your area, allowing you to gauge where you're at, in relation to the norm. Other websites that offer similar services are See My Personality and Test Color.

Essentially, it's important to remember that you'll only be able to experience financial growth if you're willing to experience personal growth too. Personal growth looks different for every single one of us, some of us need to work on our tempers in order to experience it, while others might have to work on their self-control, self-esteem, confidence, or assertiveness to do the same.

Chapter 5:

Choose Your Method

Your personality type, as well as your personal preferences and goals, will help you to determine the house flipping method that you're going to follow. There are three main house flipping techniques, low-volume to high-net investing, high-volume to low-net investing, and phone call flipping. Luckily they're all incredibly straightforward and easy to understand, but that doesn't mean that every one of them will be suitable for you.

Of course, there's no rule that states that you need to pick a strategy and stick with it until the end of days. You could theoretically cycle through these until you find the one that you liked most, or you could spend the rest of your real estate career making use of a different strategy with every flip.

The main reason why it is important to choose a strategy is to avoid aimless buying and selling. Having a plan normally gives you a clear map to follow in order to meet your goals, and it's no different in the realm of property. If you know that you're going to specialize in flipping bargain homes, it's easier to know what kind of properties to look out for. The same principle applies if you're going to be wholesaling or specializing in high-end properties.

The Low-volume, High-net Investor

This technique involves only flipping one or two houses a year. Sounds great, doesn't it? The only downside is that you need to flip incredibly expensive properties in order to make enough money to live off of if it's your goal to financially sustain yourself by flipping properties alone. This can be problematic because you generally need access to a substantial loan and initial investment capital to be able to buy expensive properties, something that's simply not attainable for most beginner house flippers (unless you're lucky enough to be the beneficiary of a wealthy trust fund).

Despite often remaining nothing but a lofty ideal, this is the strategy that most house flippers hope to eventually embody simply because it allows you to free up most of your time for more enjoyable pursuits (like yachting in the Bahamas).

Financial obstacles aside, low-volume to high-net investing is best suited to ambitious risk-takers who are confident in themselves and their abilities (enough so to sell property to influential or wealthy clients). The Myers-Briggs system would describe this personality type as being ESTP.

While you're working towards having enough money to employ this flipping strategy, you should also work towards taking on some of the personality traits that are known to pair well with it.

The Higher-volume, Lower-net Investor

This is the strategy that the majority of house flippers make use of. It's also the easiest and most practical strategy, so it's not hard to understand why it's the most popular. High-volume to low-net flipping involves flipping more than four or five houses every single year. These houses are often inexpensive or undervalued so flippers are able to make a small and fast profit from investing in each of them.

You don't need half as much money to participate in high-volume to low-net investing as you do to be able to make use of low-volume to high-net investing. So this strategy is the one to employ if you're still busy working your way up to being able to afford low-volume to high-net investing.

If you're someone who is highly organized, goal-oriented, determined, and hard-working, then you're the perfect kind of person to make use of this strategy. The Myers-Briggs system would classify someone with these traits as an ENTJ. If you belong to this personality group, you're in the perfect position to make millions by consistently trading low- to mid-level homes.

The most significant downside to this technique is that you need to commit a good amount of time to executing it if you'd like to make a living off of house flipping alone. This boils down to the fact that you need to flip a higher number of properties in order to make enough money if you're making use of this method. Flipping more properties naturally means liaising with more contractors, doing more renovations, offering more viewings, and attending to more inquiries.

The amount of time you need to dedicate to flipping houses when you're making use of high-volume to low-net investing means that this technique is largely incompatible with part-timers, as you'll likely need to commit an entire working day to flipping activities if you'd like to make money by using this strategy. Leaving your regular employment to pursue your real estate dreams is a daunting task even for the most self-assured property aficionados out there, but unfortunately it's often a necessary evil on the path to real estate success.

The Phone Call Flipper

Phone call flippers are delegators, not doers. They prefer to assign tasks to others instead of taking a more hands-on approach to renovations, marketing or sales. They're so averse to physically playing a role in the business of flipping that they often make use of wholesaling. Wholesaling is a tricky house flipping technique that involves signing a contract to buy a house, but then reassigning this contract to a different buyer before the transaction is concluded for a fee.

An example of this would be if you saw a run-down property, with lots of potential, for sale for $150,000, and signed a contract of sale as if to acquire it, only to 'sell' this contract to a new buyer for, $40,000 (without ever having to pay the initially contracted $150,000). Phone call flippers also generally prefer making use of real estate agents when not involved in wholesaling, as doing so allows them to keep the distance that they so desperately crave.

People who make use of this strategy tend to be categorized by the Myers-Briggs personality system as INTJ-types. This means that if you tend to be a thinker rather than a doer, if you consider yourself an introvert, and if you're a logical, concise person, then phone call flipping might be the perfect house flipping strategy for you. It will allow you to distance yourself from the hustle and bustle of real estate without having to distance yourself from its possible profits.

Luckily, you don't need to have a lot of investment capital at your disposal in order to be a phone call flipper (no more than you'd need for high-volume to low-net investing, anyway). One might even argue that wholesaling, which is simply a form of phone call flipping, is the most penny wise way to start flipping houses because you technically do not need any start-up capital to get going. All you need to be able to make money from wholesaling, is the ability to resell contracts of sale that have already been negotiated before their closing dates, something that's a lot easier to acquire than hundreds of thousands of dollars are.

Chapter 6:

Apply Your Strategy

By this point, you should have a relatively good idea of the strategy you're planning to follow, the kind of properties you're interested in investing in, the locations you'd like to target your efforts, the extent and type of renovations and repairs that you're willing to commit to, your legal obligations as a house flipper, and investment pitfalls that you should try to avoid. All that's left to do is to buy, and consequently sell, your first investment property.

You might have all of the theoretical house flipping knowledge in the world, but if you don't have the know-how to conclude property transactions in a profitable way then you'll never be a real estate mogul. Fortunately, it's not rocket science to learn how to conduct profitable property transactions, and you should be able to master doing so in a relatively short period of time with a little bit of determination and a good dose of grit.

You're close to concluding your journey to becoming a property investor, the finish line is in sight. If you're willing to take the final leap, and to put your money where your mouth is by making a down payment on your first investment house, you'll be well on your way to affording that yacht in the Bahamas that you've always dreamed of owning (or putting your kids through college, if your financial aspirations hit a little closer to home).

Don't worry, I'm not about to drop you in the deep end with no idea where to start. Learning about property transactions is not only easy, it's enjoyable too.

The Process of Buying Your First Investment Property

The first step to buying your very first investment home is making an offer. Many first time homeowners mistakenly think that making an offer is as easy as simply suggesting an amount to the seller, but unfortunately it's not that easy. To make an offer, you need to submit a suggested purchase price to the seller, along with the date for closing that you have in mind, as well as proof of financing (or proof of your bank balance if you're not buying on credit), in writing. If you're making use of a real estate agent's services, they'll help you to word and format your offer.

One of the golden rules of house flipping is never to offer the asking price of the property, you should always offer ten- or twenty-thousand dollars less than what the property was advertised for. Sellers are often desperate to offload their properties, so they'll normally be willing to accept a lower offer, and even when they're not, many anticipate that buyers will try to low-ball them on the offer, and consequently advertise the property for more than they're *really* expecting to get anyway.

A weird trick that seems to work for some reason is avoiding offering a round purchase sum like $250,000, and opting instead to offer a less uniform sum like $252,255. Psychologists suggest that buyers might be more likely to accept an offer on a purchase price that's an odd number because our brains register it as being much higher than it actually is. It's worth a try, especially considering that you might be competing with other bidders.

If you find a property that really piques your interest, it's important to make an offer on it as soon as possible, especially if it's well-priced. It's important to be mindful of the fact that you're not the only potential buyer out there. If you wait too long to make an offer, someone else might beat you to it and buy the house out from underneath you. You might also want to consider penning a personal letter to the seller to submit alongside your offer. There's a chance that the seller might receive more than one offer almost simultaneously and sending a letter alongside your offer expressing your sincere interest can help you to stand out as the more favorable candidate. Sometimes doing that little bit of extra effort can go a long way.

So, you've made an offer on your first investment property and it has been accepted, what now? Well, the next part of the process is called 'closing.' Your closing has to be conducted by an attorney or a title company, and essentially involves the transfer of the cost price of the property into the seller's account, and the transfer of the property's title deed into your name. At the end of closing, you're the rightful owner of the property and the seller is significantly richer. If you're making use of a loan to finance the purchase of the property, closing is also when the lending company will require you to sign off, once and for all, on the related mortgage note.

The attorney or title company involved will let you know when it's time to close on the deal, at which point they'll set up a meeting with you and the seller. This meeting will likely see the seller handing you the keys to the property as well as you receiving its title deed. There are a number of documents that you should take to a closing meeting, to make it easier for your attorney or title company to conclude the transaction, these are:

- A valid copy of one of your identification documents (like your driving license)
- Documents pertaining to negotiations on the selling price of the property
- Your mortgage documents and contracts
- Home inspection and pest inspection reports
- A cashier's check to the value of the property's down payment (or total cost if you're not buying it on credit) and that also includes any associated closing costs

Don't be startled when you show up to the closing meeting and it looks like a meeting of parliament. There are a lot of players involved in the closing of a property transaction. Any closing meeting is guaranteed to be well attended: you'll be there, the seller will be there, the closing attorney or a title company representative will be there, a representative from the company who issued your mortgage will be there, and there might even be a notary to certify all of the relevant documents. There's no reason to be intimidated by the size of the meeting, after all you're all there for the same reason—to conclude the deal.

You should try to work the cost of closing on a deal into your original budget because it can be quite pricey, and can consequently affect your profit margins if you're not careful. *USA Today* recently ran a poll among its readers that found that you should budget an extra

$13,000 for the closing costs of a property that is worth about $200,000 (which is the price range that most house flippers operate). The problem with closing costs is that you generally won't know exactly what they'll be until just before closing when you're handed an HUD-1 form. This is a form that will be issued by the institution that is facilitating your mortgage. It contains a summary of all of the costs (along with who needs to pay them you or the seller), that need to be settled before closing can take place. It will give you an exact number that you have to pay during the closing meeting in order to conclude the transaction.

Once the transaction is closed, the property is legally yours, and you can finally dive head first into your improvements, repairs, and renovations. You want to avoid making any improvements to a property before the sale has been completely concluded, even if the seller allows or encourages it. It's not reasonable to take the risk of spending money on a property if there's still a chance that the sale might not go through or be successful. Imagine the incredible legal hassle that would ensue if you were to reshingle the roof of a property only to have the seller back out of the sale at the last minute, leaving you financially poorer and the seller one shiny new roof richer.

The Process of Selling Your First Investment Property

Once you've made the desired improvements to your investment property, it's time to start marketing it. But first you need to decide whether or not you want to sell it by making use of a real estate agent. I highly recommend that you do make use of a real estate agent simply because they're experienced professionals who are likely to be able to help you find a buyer for your house within the blink of an eye. However, it is possible to sell your house without making use of one, and many house flippers do indeed choose to make use of this option.

The reason why they opt to do this boils down to a question of savings. Most real estate agents charge 6% commission, that means that if you'd like to sell a home for $200,000, they'd market it for $212,000, and take $12,000 of the sale's price upon closing. That's $12,000 that could have been in your pocket instead. The problem with trying to sell a property without a real estate agent, is that it takes a good deal of commitment and dedication in order to do it within a reasonable time frame (and you do want to do it in a reasonable time frame because the longer your investment property remains unsold, the more rates and taxes you'll end up having to pay on it).

Without a real estate agent to take the lead, you'll have to do all of your advertising and marketing yourself. You'll have to communicate with anyone that has queries or questions about the property, and you'll have to take full responsibility for viewings, including showing potential buyers around your investment property. You'll have to draw up the contract of sale (unless you hire a real estate attorney to help you), and you may have to communicate with the deed's office and the contracted title company.

In short, you basically need a short course on selling houses in order to be able to proceed without a real estate agent and it might still not be worth it in the long run. A study that was conducted two years ago by the National Association of Realtors' found that self-sold homes sold for more than $60,000 less than those that were marketed and sold by real estate agents.

The next step is to start advertising your investment property. If you're making use of a real estate agent, it's not necessary (although I'm sure they'd appreciate the help). However, if you're not making use of a real estate agent, you're going to need to advertise like crazy. A good place to start is on your own social media accounts, you never know which of your old high school buddies might be in the market for a brand-new family home.

Once you've sufficiently flooded your own Twitter and Facebook accounts with advertisements for your investment property, it's time to start posting them to some other property listing websites. Some of the best ones that are entirely free to use for private sellers are Craigslist, FindMyRoof, Oodle, Fizber, Letgo, ForSaleByOwner, and Connected Investors. Properly advertising your investment property takes more than just posting three pictures from Google Maps with a five-word description and a price tag. It takes a bit more finesse than that. Real estate agents are normally trained to write stellar property listings, a skill you'll have to acquire on your own if you're winging it alone.

Luckily, there are a few golden rules for writing house listings that will enable you to write listings that are on par with those of even the best real estate agents. First, it's crucial to ensure that your spelling and grammar are correct in any listing that you've written. You want potential buyers to take you seriously as a real estate professional, and you make it hard for them to do so if your advertisement is riddled with language errors. Putting a listing through a language checker like Grammarly.com will help you to pick up any spelling or grammatical errors before publishing them to your social media accounts or real estate websites.

Secondly, you want to make sure that the photographs of the property that you're using are flattering. To do this you'll need to get your hands on a professional quality camera with a wide angle lens (your cellphone's camera simply won't do). A wide angle lens is a crucial part of any real estate photographer's toolkit because it allows you to photograph a room in its entirety instead of having to choose a specific wall or corner to photograph. You might also want to consider investing in a tripod, as making use of one will drastically increase the quality of your photographs.

Before getting started you should clean up and declutter the house. Remember to make sure that any pets or people are out of frame before taking any photographs, you might think that your puppy is adorable, but the chances are pretty good that potential buyers don't want to see him or her. It's also important to make sure that you take photographs from flattering angles, making sure to highlight your homes positive features (like new kitchen countertops), and being sure not to photograph any less flattering features (like chipping or flaking paint, an overgrown garden, or stains on the ceiling).

Most real estate photographers also swear by 'staging' a house before photographing it (and studies support this notion, showing that staged homes sell for approximately 5% more than their unstaged counterparts). 'Staging' a house for photographs means adding certain elements to a room in order to make it look more attractive in photographs. Some of the most popular staging techniques are putting crisp white towels over bathroom rails, placing high-class bedding on beds (along with a small horde of decorative pillows), and fully setting dining room tables (including suitable centerpieces). Staging devices make it easier for potential buyers to imagine living in your investment property, which makes them more likely to book a viewing.

The timing of your photos also makes a notable difference. If you're photographing the inside of a house, you should wait until about midday, when the sun is at its brightest, to take any snapshots. You want to give potential buyers the impression that your investment property gets more than enough natural light, and that living in it won't be like living in a cave. If you're photographing the outside of a house or its garden, you should wait until just before sunset on a very pleasant, sunny day. The light is too bright outside, in the morning or at midday, to take the kind of photographs outside that will blow potential buyers away. In fact, all that you'll accomplish if you try to do it then, is snapping shots of an overexposed garden with colors that will be washed out and dull.

Once you've considered all of the aforementioned aspects and taken the perfect photographs, it's time to do some editing. Learning how to use Adobe Lightroom or Photoshop can take months, so it's fortunate that there's an easier way to get your photographs looking magazine ready - Brownie Box. Brownie Box is an online service that allows customers to submit photographs and, for about $2, they'll turn them into the best images that they can possibly be. Any professional photographer will tell you that the difference between an award-winning photograph and a mediocre one is its editing, so it's highly advised that you don't skip this step.

Thirdly, you should read a couple of professional property listings to get a feel for how they're written. Your property listing's description should be both informative and alluring. Consequently, it needs to contain basic information like the number of bedrooms, bathrooms, garages, and living areas that your investment property has, the size of the house in square foot, and the size of the lot that the house is built on. But you need to describe it in such a way that it sounds like an advertisement and not a clinical technical analysis.

Although the writing of your property listing's description needs to be appealing, it's important not to go overboard with your use of adjectives. Adding strings of adjectives onto each other can leave potential buyers with the impression that you're either unprofessional or overeager to sell the property (and you never want to seem overeager or else potential buyers might try to low ball you on their offers). Ideally you should also try to avoid using words that have well known negative connotations in the real estate world, like cozy (which is often just code for tiny), traditional (which often means outdated), 'fixer-upper' (which normally means 'in bad shape'), or cheap (nobody wants to think that they're being cheap when they're investing in property).

While certain words may send potential buyers running for the hills, studies have also found that certain words compel potential buyers to book viewings too. Words and terms like "luxurious," "top quality," "classy finishes," and "newly renovated" have all been found to be highly attractive to those who are looking to purchase a house. It's also important to try to keep your property listing's description as short, sweet, and to-the-point as possible. Generally speaking, people are lazy readers. Potential buyers are unlikely to read more than one or two paragraphs of information pertaining to the property that you're trying to sell. So there's no point in penning a small book on the subject in hopes of luring anyone in.

An example of a good property listing description would be:

"Luxurious three bedroom home for sale, with spacious living areas, a newly renovated kitchen, and located in a safe neighborhood. All 1,200 square foot of it has recently been repainted. A large garden means that it's an entertainer's paradise. Pull your car into one of the two beautiful attached garages and move right in. Its classy finishes and updated comforts will make you feel right at home."

This is an example of a good property description because it lists some of the property's most important features without becoming verbose in its description of them. Did you notice how I managed to work in some of those 'magic' words and terms we spoke about earlier?

An example of a bad property listing would be:

"Three-bedroom house, big garden, two garages, nice kitchen, good living areas, traditional finishings, cozy. Going cheap and needs some attention."

This example is riddled with words that are known to drive off potential buyers. It's too short, and entirely devoid of any descriptive language that could allow potential buyers to imagine the best possible version of your investment property. Instead, this kind of advertisement will surely leave them feeling that the seller isn't motivated to sell or that the property doesn't offer the same kind of bang for your buck that its counterparts do.

You might start receiving responses on your advertisement within minutes of posting it on the internet (although it's just as likely that you'll wait days before anyone shows any interest). At this point you need to be ready to start scheduling viewings with potential buyers. A viewing is when potential buyers come to look at the property that you have for sale. They'll expect to be allowed to see the entire lot, as well as every room in the house. Some of them might even check that the toilets flush, open cupboards to inspect them, or ask to switch on the air conditioning system. You need to be prepared for every possible eventuality if you really want to impress them.

There are a few simple things that you can do to get your property viewing ready. You should always start by giving the entire house a deep clean, including cleaning carpets, washing walls, pressure-washing the driveway and garage floor, washing windows, cleaning out inbuilt storage spaces, cleaning out any inbuilt light fixtures, cleaning out gutters, pulling out any weeds in the garden, mowing the lawn, and raking up any leaves or other garden waste.

Next, you should remove any personal effects like photos of family and friends, trinkets and children's toys. Potential buyers have to be able to picture themselves living in your investment property, and you make it difficult for them to do so if you leave them little reminders of your family all around the house. Another pro-tip is to find somewhere else for your pets to stay (especially free-roaming pets) when your house is being viewed. I'm a dog lover myself, so I hate to even make this suggestion, but unfortunately, you may come across potential buyers who are allergic to pet hair or who are deathly afraid of your pets. It'll be less stressful for Fluffy too, to be somewhere else when strangers are combing through his or her house (moves are stressful enough for pets).

You should also try to remove any sources of unpleasant smells or odors in your investment property before taking anyone through it for a viewing such as, cat litter boxes, dead leaves and debris produced by potted plants, pet cages or enclosures, and dirty dishes (and no, simply putting them in the sink doesn't count). Our sense of smell is one of the most special ways that we human beings commit moments to memory, so you want to ensure that the smell that potential buyers associate with your house is a pleasant one.

Some house flippers swear by burning scented candles or incense during a viewing, while others believe that you can create that 'homey' feeling we all know and love by stuffing a load of baking bread into the oven just before potential buyers arrive for a viewing (most of our brains associate the smell of baking bread with either our parents or our grandparents, solid memories to build your viewing experience on).

There's only one thing viewers seem to hate more than a stinky house, and that's a dark house. You should try to make your home as light as possible for any potential buyers that come to look at it. This can usually be accomplished by opening all of the house's blinds and curtains, but if the property doesn't get a lot of natural sunlight, you may have to resort to making use of artificial lighting. Switch on a couple of strategic lights in your home (good ones include hallway lights, bathroom lights, and bedroom lights). Nobody wants to feel like they live in a badger hole, so it's understandable why potential buyers might be put off if they get the impression that your property is perpetually dark and devoid of sunlight.

You'll start a viewing by welcoming the potential buyer (or buyers) to the property. You may choose to briefly show them around the house while discussing its history and highlighting its most desirable elements. But thereafter, you should afford the viewer the opportunity to walk around the house and surrounding property on their own. When surveyed, almost all potential buyers indicated that they were more likely to make an offer on a property if they were allowed to inspect it on their own. It's very easy to be tempted to follow viewers around anywhere (who really wants strangers looking around their house unaccompanied?), but it's simply something you'll have to make peace with doing if you're serious about selling your investment property as soon as possible.

Once the viewer has had a chance to wander around the house and lot unaccompanied, you should meet back up with them and afford them the opportunity to ask you any questions they may have pertaining to the property. It's likely that they won't have any questions for you at this point, although you should make sure that you give them your contact details and reassure them that they can contact you at any time should any questions or queries arise. A normal house viewing normally only takes about 30 minutes to complete, although some viewers can take much longer.

It's absolutely crucial that you allow viewers to take their time and that you don't give them the impression that you're trying to rush them to finish. Potential buyers are preparing to spend a small fortune on purchasing your property, so try to give them a pleasant viewing experience. Once the viewing is over, you should wait a couple of hours, and then send the viewer an email or text message thanking them for their interest in your property and inviting them to reach out with any questions that they may have. However, it's important not to badger potential buyers, so once this message is sent, you should refrain from contacting them again unless they contact you first.

You'll probably get your first offer after conducting your first couple of viewings, you might even get more than one. The golden rule of receiving offers is this: never go with the first one. You might be eager to see the fruits of your labor, which makes it hard to resist taking the first offer you receive, but if you're simply willing to exercise a measure of self-control and patience, you'll surely find that you're able to increase your profit margins by thoroughly scrutinizing all of the offers that you get.

First, you should avoid accepting offers that are far below your asking price. Giving too much leeway on your planned sale price is one of the easiest ways to lose money, so don't do it. Secondly, you should understand the value of cash offers. Cash offers are more likely to result in a sale because they mean that the potential buyer doesn't have to face the hurdle of securing financing. It also means that the sale will be concluded faster because you don't have to wait for a third party to come to the table to make it happen (consequently you'll have the proceeds from the sale in your pocket sooner). Considering everything, it's sometimes a good move to take a cash offer over a credit offer, even if it is a little bit lower than the latter.

Some buyers may also add conditions to their offer in an attempt to make it more attractive to you, like foregoing an inspection, allowing you to stay on even after the sale has been concluded, or putting down a portion of the sales price immediately to show you how serious they are about purchasing the property. Your goal should be to review at least two offers before selecting one, and only choosing an offer which meets the minimum amount that you need to sell for in order to make a profit. Although, you'd ideally select one with even more perks than that.

Of course, you can make a counteroffer on any offer that you receive. Counteroffers are changes that you suggest making to a potential buyer's offer, with the intention of accepting the offer should they accept the suggested changes. For example, a potential buyer might offer you $200,000 for a property that you advertised for $250,000. You may be unable (or rightfully unwilling) to accept an offer like $200,000, at which point you would approach the potential buyer and make a counteroffer stating that they'd need to increase their bid price to $225,000. You don't have to accept any offers that you get exactly as they're made, you're allowed (and encouraged) to negotiate and discuss them with the potential buyers that made them. You can always try to charm your way into a larger profit margin.

Once you and a potential buyer agree on the terms and conditions of sale, you're said to be 'contracted in' or 'under contract.' Under normal circumstances, the buyer then has a 'due diligence' period of about 10 days. This time period essentially allows the buyer to back out of the sale without reason during those ten days, although its actual purpose is to allow the buyer time to conduct any inspections that they'd like to have done before fully committing to the sale. If your potential buyer is making use of financing in order to conclude the sale, your property will also likely be appraised by their financing institution during this time. Additionally, you might also have the title company knocking on your door to inspect your property for any applicable liens before permitting its sale. In short, you should be ready to be bombarded by visitors, all looking to poke and prod at your investment property.

If you're lucky, you should get to 'closing day' a week or two after exiting the due diligence period. If you're making use of a real estate attorney or a real estate agent, you won't even have to be at the conclusionary meeting on closing day. But if you're tackling the sale of your investment property solo, you'll need to be there on the day to sign the contract, deed, and transfer of ownership documents that are needed to finalize and register the sale. The closing day meeting is generally conducted between the buyer, the seller (or their representatives), a representative from the title company, and a representative from the lending company (where applicable). Once this meeting has been concluded, the transfer of ownership is complete and the payment of the sale price should be pending to be paid into your account.

Selling your first investment property is really that easy. If you follow my instructions to a tee, I guarantee that you'll be well on your way to becoming a real estate tycoon. Make an effort to present your property well (in person and online), and you'll have potential buyers knocking down your door, begging you to sell them your property. Offers will be flooding in so fast that you'll struggle to keep up with them.

Tips and Tricks for Cutting Costs

At the end of the day, how much money you'll be able to make by flipping houses depends entirely on your ability to spend as little money as possible on their renovations before reselling them. I know it sounds cheap (and nobody likes to sound cheap), but if you're spending $30,000 more than necessary on renovations before offloading your investment property, you're essentially just robbing yourself of $30,000 worth of profit. Your mission shouldn't be to turn every home that you encounter into your dream house, it should be to turn every home that you encounter into a marketable asset. Something doesn't need to be perfect in order to be marketable; in fact, many a dream has been killed by avid perfectionism. When it comes to renovations and the costs associated with house flipping, sometimes you'll have to settle for 'good enough' and give up on trying to get to 'perfect.'

Seasoned house flippers generally know quite a few tips and tricks to cut costs, some of which have been passed down to them by mentors, while others have been learned through years of hard-earned experience. Luckily for you, I'm going to save you decades worth of tears in a few short paragraphs on well-known cost-cutting measures.

To start with, if you ever find yourself holding on to a property longer than you expected to, then you could consider renting it out to avoid the overall cost of the flip increasing due to accruing utilities, rates, levies, and taxes. Renters aren't ideal because they can be off-putting to potential buyers, but if your investment property has been on the market for months, I highly recommend you find renters to help recover some of your already growing losses. Additionally, if the property that you're flipping is in an area where crime is very prevalent, taking on renters can ensure that your property isn't damaged and fixtures aren't stolen while it's for sale.

Another top trick is to time your property purchases in such a way that all of (or most of) your renovations take place in the winter. Winter is called the 'off season' in the world of real estate. This is largely because properties don't sell well in winter (especially in the colder Northern states), which in turn lowers the demand for building materials and construction-related labor. If you know anything about the economy, you know that supply and demand are the two major factors when it comes to determining the value of a commodity. A drastic drop in demand, such as is experienced in the realm of real estate in winter, drives prices down to far below their normal rate.

What this means for you, as a house flipper, is that you'll be able to buy the supplies to make repairs and do renovations, at a significantly lower price in the off season. In correlation with this, you'll also find that contractors and builders are willing to do work for a lot cheaper than they usually are. We all prefer to remain snuggled up in bed with a good book or a whimsical movie on frosty winter days, but the truth is that you're probably better off using them to make all of the necessary changes to your investment properties before putting them back on the market.

Speaking of inexpensive contractors, another money-savvy move to make is to consider employing college kids and moonlighters as laborers. Moonlighters are people who take on projects for a fee, but who actually have a different (often entirely unrelated) full-time occupation. Both moonlighters and college kids are normally willing to work for a lot less than seasoned professionals are because they're looking to pick up work experience. The only downside to making use of their services is that quality isn't always guaranteed. Moonlighters and college kids are willing to work for cheaper because they're less knowledgeable, and while this isn't always a problem it certainly becomes one when things start heading south and you start noticing problems.

If you've decided to make use of the high-volume to low-net house flipping strategy, you can also save yourself a pretty penny by renovating and repairing all of the houses currently in your possession, at the same time. That way you can make use of bulk discounts, and if you're making use of contractors they'll probably be willing to give you a better price if you're willing to make use of their services for multiple separate contracts.

The only pitfall I'd warn you to be cautious of, when you're trying to save money while flipping houses, is not to resort to making use of low-quality building materials in an attempt to lower your costs. Ultimately, you have a legal and moral obligation to give buyers a safe, comfortable home, and using subpar building materials is often a health risk, and is unsightly too. That isn't to say that you can't take a couple of shortcuts while renovating your investment property. Some of the well-known cost-saving measures employed by successful house flippers include repainting cabinets and counters instead of replacing them (or only replacing their doors if they're really looking worse for wear), and upcycling materials by making use of previously loved fixtures, tiles, bricks, woodwork, and countertops (as long as they're still in acceptable condition).

There are also some ways that you can save money during the acquisition process, the easiest of which is negotiating with the real estate agent regarding their commission fee. Most real estate agents charge a commission fee of between three and six percent of the property's purchase price, and many can be convinced to take a little less to make a quick sale. They will usually be more flexible on their fee if you're making a cash offer instead of buying through a lending institution.

Regardless of the kind of offer you're about to make, it's always worth finding out if the real estate agent is willing to negotiate. It's also a good idea to consider a number of title companies to make use of, before putting your heart on any single one, to ensure that you're getting value for your money. Title companies' charges and services tend to vary greatly, which makes it even more important to compare a few before going ahead with the transaction.

Saving money during a house flip is all about using logic to surmise which costs can reasonably be cut and which contractors are open to negotiation. Your attempts at haggling down real estate agents and builders might be a bit shaky (or even unsuccessful) in the beginning, but you'll soon find that experience makes it easy to spot parties that are open to discuss their fees and rates.

Conclusion

Studies have shown that nine-tenths of all American millionaires have made property investments a part of their financial portfolios. Property is one of those assets that is always a good idea to invest in, regardless of your intentions or financial position. Unlike many other investment assets, it hardly ever substantially devalues (except for under exceptional circumstances), and it's normally liquid enough to be turned back into cash within a reasonable amount of time.

Of course, flipping houses is a special kind of property investing, one that's reserved for the extra-ambitious, for those that are destined to rise out of their current financial rank. The commitment that you've shown to learning about this kind of property investing proves that you're one of those people, one of the special few that are destined for something more, something better. And you deserve it. You deserve the kind of financial freedom that will allow you to live the life that you've always wanted, and to provide your family with the quality of life you've always wanted to offer them.

Reading this book is a good start, but you now need to put your plan into action. I urge you to start looking at your finances immediately to try to determine how much you can afford to spend on an investment property. As a matter of fact, why don't you put aside an hour or two today to start contacting lending companies to find out if you prequalify for a loan. Don't postpone your dreams.

Postponing your dreams means postponing living the kind of life that you deserve to live to a later, undetermined date. The second that you're in the position to put money down on a property, do it. Don't spend months searching for 'the one.' 'The one' is the first one you spot, that would result in a profitable flip and is within your price range. If you get started today, you could be sitting pretty before the end of a year, so why wait? With this book in hand, you have all of the knowledge you need to kick start your house flipping career. If you implement all of the advice shared between these pages, you'll find yourself watching your bank account explode in no time. You could spend next summer on a private Greek island, reminiscing about the day that you decided to pick up a three-hour guide to house flipping.

As this is likely one of the last books you'll read before becoming a real estate millionaire, why don't you leave a review on this book detailing what your house flipping financial goals are? That way, you'll have something interesting to quote when you're writing your autobiography, passing property investment knowledge on to the next generation. It'll also give you a way to track your progress, as you'll be able to look back on your initial financial goals and compare them to your current financial position.

References

3 Legal Risks of House Flipping. (n.d.). Findlaw. https://blogs.findlaw.com/law_and_life/2018/04/3-legal-risks-of-house-flipping.html

3 Ways to Flip Houses With No Money Down. (2019, February 6). Fit Small Business. https://fitsmallbusiness.com/flipping-houses-with-no-money/

4 Excellent House Flipping Exit Strategies You Should Try | House Flipping School. (n.d.). https://houseflippingschool.com/excellent-house-flipping-exit-strategies/

7 Ways To Flip Houses With No Money In 2019. (2019, June 21). FortuneBuilders. https://www.fortunebuilders.com/how-to-flip-houses-with-no-money/

33 Pro Tips on How to Flip a House for Maximum Profit. (2019, February 27). Fit Small Business. https://fitsmallbusiness.com/how-to-flip-a-house-tips/

52 Essential real estate terms you should know | Opendoor. (2019, October 17). Opendoor.

https://www.opendoor.com/w/blog/real-estate-terms-you-should-know

ATTOM Data Solutions. (n.d.). Trend Chart Home Flipping. In *PRNewsWire.com.* https://mma.prnewswire.com/media/1179055/ATTOM_Data_Solutions_US_Home_Flipping_Trends.jpg?p=publish&w=950

Best Deal Ever Show #12: Millionaire by Age 30 on only 3 Houses! (n.d.). Www.Biggerpockets.Com. https://www.biggerpockets.com/blog/best-deal-ever-12-millionaire-by-30-from-3-houses

Blakeley, J. (2017, June 21). *A Brief Guide to Understanding Sun Exposures.* Architectural Digest; Architectural Digest. https://www.architecturaldigest.com/story/sun-exposures-lighting-guide-tips

Business Dictionary Image. (n.d.). In *Pxfuel.com.* https://p1.pxfuel.com/preview/795/793/109/dictionary-text-definition-business.jpg

Calculator. (n.d.). In *Wallpaperflare.com.* https://c1.wallpaperflare.com/preview/482/958/402/accountant-accounting-adviser-advisor.jpg

Can I Sue My Home Seller for Defects Found Post-Closing? (n.d.). Www.Lawyers.Com. https://www.lawyers.com/legal-info/real-estate/residential-real-estate-own-keep/can-i-sue-my-home-seller-for-defects-found-post-closing.html

Developing "Character": Learning How to Stand Your Ground. (n.d.). Www.Mindtools.Com. https://www.mindtools.com/pages/article/newCS_81.htm

Dictionary Reference. (n.d.). In *pxhere.com.* https://c.pxhere.com/photos/9f/cb/dictionary_reference_book_learning_meaning_knowledge_text_education_information-535832.jpg!d

Early 1980s Recession. (2020, June 11). Wikipedia. https://en.wikipedia.org/wiki/Early_1980s_recession#:~:text=The%20early%201980s%20recession%20in

Federal Housing Administration Loan – FHA Loan – Definition. (2019). Investopedia. https://www.investopedia.com/terms/f/fhaloan.asp

Fix & Flip Loans: The 5 Best Fix & Flip Financing Options. (2020, March 24). Fit Small Business. https://fitsmallbusiness.com/fix-and-flip-loans/

Flipping. (2020, May 27). Wikipedia. https://en.wikipedia.org/wiki/Flipping

Flipping Homes: 11 Ways to Cut Renovation Costs. (n.d.). Dummies. https://www.dummies.com/personal-finance/real-estate-investing/flipping-houses/flipping-homes-11-ways-to-cut-renovation-costs/

Flipping Houses for a Living: The 5 Phases of Every Flip. (2018, May 18). Connected Investors Blog. https://connectedinvestors.com/blog/flipping-houses-living/

Flipping Houses for Beginners: 6 Mistakes to Avoid. (2018, October 9). LendingHome Blog. https://www.lendinghome.com/blog/flipping-houses-for-beginners-6-mistakes-to-avoid/

Flipping Houses For Dummies Cheat Sheet. (n.d.). Dummies. https://www.dummies.com/personal-finance/real-estate-investing/flipping-houses/flipping-houses-for-dummies-cheat-sheet/

Flipping Houses: The Ultimate Step by Step Guide. (n.d.). Www.Biggerpockets.Com. https://www.biggerpockets.com/blog/2014-01-07-flipping-houses

For Sale Sign In Front of House. (n.d.). In *Flickr.com.* https://live.staticflickr.com/3784/11705392445_86c98890bc_b.jp

For Sale Signs. (n.d.). In *Needpix.com.* https://storage.needpix.com/rsynced_images/1-1207418920VmzY.jpg

From Bookkeeper to Real Estate Millionaire in 11 Years. (2018, October 29). Coach Carson. https://www.coachcarson.com/bookkeeper-to-millionaire/

Hand On Door Handle. (n.d.). In *Pxfuel.com.* https://p1.pxfuel.com/preview/160/895/781/house-key-house-keys-real-estate-building-door.jpg

Hess, A. (2017, February 28). *Self-made millionaire bought his first flip while making only 40000.* Www.Cnbc.Com. https://www.cnbc.com/2017/02/28/self-made-millionaire-bought-his-first-flip-while-making-only-40000.html

House and Keys. (n.d.). In *Pxfuel.com.* https://p1.pxfuel.com/preview/831/415/584/build-a-house-house-for-sale-house-for-rent-property-building-construction.jpg

House Flipping Formulas. (n.d.). Www.Flipperforce.Com. https://www.flipperforce.com/house-flipping-formulas

House Flipping Slang Deciphered: From Bird Dogs to Bene. (2016, January 18). Real Estate News and Advice | Realtor.Com®. https://www.realtor.com/advice/buy/flipping-glossary-slang-lingo/

House Flipping Stats - Where the Profits Are. (2017, December 18). Connected Investors Blog. https://connectedinvestors.com/blog/house-flipping-stats/

House On Laptop. (n.d.). In *Pxfuel.com.* https://p1.pxfuel.com/preview/848/480/964/house-keys-security-door-key-ssl-real-estate-close.jpg

How Much Can You Make Flipping Houses? The Answer May Surprise You. (2019, July 31). HomeLight Blog. https://www.homelight.com/blog/how-much-can-you-make-flipping-houses/

How to Flip a House. (2016). Daveramsey.Com. https://www.daveramsey.com/blog/how-to-flip-a-house

How to Flip a House With No Money. (2019, October 28). Nav. https://www.nav.com/blog/how-to-flip-a-house-with-no-money-297869/

How to Get Preapproved For a Mortgage. (n.d.). NerdWallet. https://www.nerdwallet.com/article/mortgages/how-to-get-a-mortgage-preapproval

How to Read a Listing | Toronto Real Estate. (2019, January 22). Pierre Carapetian Group. https://pierrecarapetian.com/how-to-read-mls-listing-sheet/

How to Read a Property Listing with Flipping in Mind. (n.d.). Dummies.

https://www.dummies.com/personal-finance/real-estate-investing/flipping-houses/how-to-read-a-property-listing-with-flipping-in-mind/

Kidd, J. (2019, August 8). *How Many Houses Can You Flip in a Year?* Flipping Prosperity. https://flippingprosperity.com/how-many-houses-can-you-flip-in-a-year/

Learning the Lingo: Architecture Edition. (2015, December 1). Real Estate News and Advice | Realtor.Com®. https://www.realtor.com/advice/buy/most-popular-architecture-styles/

Man Jumping In Front Of House. (n.d.). In *Pexels.com.* https://images.pexels.com/photos/33343/building-joy-planning-plans.jpg?auto=compress&cs=tinysrgb&dpr=2&h=650&w=940

Man Taking Phonecall. (n.d.). In *Pexels.com.* https://images.pexels.com/photos/859264/pexels-photo-859264.jpeg?auto=compress&cs=tinysrgb&dpr=2&h=650&w=940

Material Defects Defined for Home Inspectors. (n.d.). Www.Nachi.Org. https://www.nachi.org/material-defects-for-home-inspectors.htm

McWhinney, J. (n.d.). *5 Mistakes That Can Make House Flipping a Flop.* Investopedia. https://www.investopedia.com/articles/mortgages-real-estate/08/house-flip.asp

Millionaire Interview: Armando Montelongo – Host of Flip This House, Real Estate Investor and Author of Flip and Grow Rich. (2011, May 23). Eventual Millionaire. https://eventualmillionaire.com/millionaire-interview-armando-montelongo-host-of-flip-house-real-estate-investor-author-of-flip-grow-rich/

Monopoly Money on Coins. (n.d.). In *Flickr.com.* https://live.staticflickr.com/5137/5474211395_8fd5618d0e_b.jpg

Nelson, L. (n.d.). *How To Sell A House By Owner | Bankrate.com.* Bankrate. https://www.bankrate.com/real-estate/how-to-sell-house-by-owner/

Person In The Mirror. (n.d.). In *Pxfuel.com.* https://p1.pxfuel.com/preview/442/931/590/mirror-hand-face-close.jpg

Piggy Bank and House. (n.d.). In *Flickr.com.* https://live.staticflickr.com/6134/5929481283_33c2e26e35_b.jpg

Pros and Cons of Flipping Houses [infographic]. (n.d.). Www.Realestatesalesllc.Com.

https://www.realestatesalesllc.com/real-estate/pros-cons-flipping-houses/

Real Estate & House Flipping Glossary. (n.d.). Www.Flipperforce.Com. https://www.flipperforce.com/real-estate-glossary

Shaw, G. (n.d.). *9 celebrities who flip homes on the side*. Insider. https://www.insider.com/celebrities-who-flip-homes-2019-7#ellen-degeneres-is-one-of-the-most-famous-celebrity-house-flippers-2

Spend Money. (n.d.). In *Flickr.com*. https://live.staticflickr.com/6106/6355818699_a9bed226f8_b.jpg

The Appraisal Profession - AI Resources | Appraisal Institute. (2018). Appraisalinstitute.Org. https://www.appraisalinstitute.org/appraisal-profession/

The Best Books on Flipping Houses. (n.d.). Millionacres. https://www.fool.com/millionacres/real-estate-investing/house-flipping/books-on-flipping-houses/

The Complete Guide to Flipping Houses From A to Z. (n.d.). InvestFourMore. https://investfourmore.com/70-rule-real-estate/

The Process of Closing on a House. (2020). Moneyunder30.Com.

https://www.moneyunder30.com/closing-on-house-process-and-costs

Thorsby, D. (2020). *The Guide to Making and Accepting an Offer on a Home.* US News & World Report; U.S. News & World Report. https://realestate.usnews.com/real-estate/articles/the-guide-to-making-and-accepting-an-offer-on-a-home

Title insurance. (2020, April 23). Wikipedia. https://en.wikipedia.org/wiki/Title_insurance#Owner

Top 5 Termite Signs to Look for in the Home | Terminix. (n.d.). Terminix.Com. https://www.terminix.com/termite-control/termite-signs/

Trondheim Houses. (n.d.). In *Pixabay.* https://cdn.pixabay.com/photo/2017/02/17/15/02/trondheim-2074284_960_720.jpg

Upside Down Reflection. (n.d.). In *Wallpaperflare.com.* https://c0.wallpaperflare.com/preview/4/986/327/broken-conceptual-cracked-glass.jpg

Vasel, K. (2018, June 5). *He made $400,000 flipping a house.* CNNMoney. https://money.cnn.com/2018/06/05/real_estate/house-flipping/index.html

Wad of Dollars. (n.d.). In *Flickr.com.* https://live.staticflickr.com/6039/6280510901_94a4e8f7e7_b.jpg

Washington Houses. (n.d.). In *Pxhere.com.* https://c.pxhere.com/photos/5a/f5/washington_dc_c_city_cities_urban_row_houses_scenic_colorful-540332.jpg!d

Weighing Scales. (n.d.). In *Piqsels.com.* https://p1.piqsels.com/preview/923/866/544/balance-justice-uplands-flea-market-old-instrument.jpg

What is My Credit Score - How to Check Your Credit - Wells Fargo. (n.d.). Www.Wellsfargo.Com. https://www.wellsfargo.com/financial-education/credit-management/check-credit-score/

Woman Reading Book. (n.d.). In *Pixnio.com.* https://pixnio.com/free-images/2017/03/13/2017-03-13-16-43-13-725x483.jpg

www.ingramcontent.com/pod-product-compliance
Ingram Content Group UK Ltd.
Pitfield, Milton Keynes, MK11 3LW, UK
UKHW010236041225
9335UKWH00016B/429